Hungary 1956 - 1986

Compiled and Edited under the direction of
István B. Gereben

Alpha Publications, Inc.
1986

Covers by Sam Maitin

Printed in the United States of America
Copyright © 1986 by Alpha Publications, Inc.
Library of Congress Catalog Number 86-51347
ISBN 0-912404-05-1

Published by Alpha Publications, Inc.
1079 DeKalb Pike, Center Square, Pennsylvania 19422
U.S.A.

Dedicated to the Freedom Fighters of 1956
and to those who carry on their struggle

ACKNOWLEDGMENTS

First and foremost, we must pay tribute to the many writers, editors, publishers, typists, and others involved in the production and dissemination of the writings on which the translations in this book are based. They sacrificed more than time and energy.

Special thanks must be expressed to the editorial committee and executives of the Coordinating Committee of Hungarian Organizations in North America, who contributed their time and effort to provide the translations, the editing, and the administrative work necessary to publish this book.

We want to acknowledge the role of Mr. Tibor Tollas, editor of *Nemzetőr,* who made the original suggestion for the publication of this book. Without his support and the example of the similar Hungarian language collection *Független* (Independent) Forum, published by *Nemzetőr,* the present volume migth not have appeared.

Special recognition and thanks are owed to the translators and editors who contributed their talents and efforts to making this volume available to the English language reader.

We want to thank Ferenc Mózsi, editor of *Szivárvány* in Chicago, Illinois, and Zoltán Zsille, editor of the *Bibó Press* in Vienna, Austria, for supplying the original publications from which the writings for this book were selected.

We want to thank Sam Maitin for his assistance in the coordination and supervision of the art work for the book.

We are grateful to the following individuals and organizations for their financial assistance:

Dr. Eugene Holly
Mrs. Lívia Jancsó
Mr. and Mrs. Thomas Keri
Dr. and Mrs. István Kriskó
Mr. and Mrs. Elek Lengyel

Mr. and Mrs. László Lukács
Mr. and Mrs. László Megyeri
Ms. Elisabeth Mauthner
Mr. and Mrs. Tibor Tollas
Ms. Zsuzsanna Vizsolyi

Aerodynamics Inspecting Company, Detroit, MI
Hungarian Association of Goteborg, Sweden
Hungarian Cultural Association of Edmonton, Canada
Hungarian Freedom Fighters Federation, Toronto Chapter
Hungarian Freedom Fighters Federation, Washington, D.C. Chapter
Hungarian Society of Massachusetts
Kőrösi Csoma Center, Tokyo, Japan
Nemzetőr, Munich, West Germany
Niagara Peninsular Canadian Hungarian Cultural and Sport Center

TABLE OF CONTENTS

FOREWORD

As Chairman and Co-Chairman of the Commission on Security and Cooperation in Europe, established to monitor and encourage compliance with the Helsinki Final Act, we are pleased to see the publication of *Defiant Voices*, a collection of writings from Hungary's "second public opinion." This volume of *samizdat,* or "self-published" material, is a valuable contribution to our knowledge of Hungary.

Those who publish *samizdat* in Hungary, or in any country where it is published, do so because they feel the need to make known to a potentially interested but somewhat isolated public those views and ideas that cannot be disseminated in the official media. To use the words of the editors of one of Hungary's major *samizdat* journals, their aim is to help "the quietly rumbling masses of people, about whom the two tiny minorities of the country's leadership and the opposition are engaged in loud argments, to form a better picture of itself." While these independent writers and publishers have made important progress to this end, this volume of *samizdat* essays will make equally important progress in helping to educate another audience, the West, on the situation in Hungary.

Western attention, particularly here in the United States, frequently passes over what is happening in Hungary and the other communist countries of East and East/Central Europe, focusing instead on events concerning the Soviet Union. This is unfortunate, because these other countries are a much greater factor in East-West relations than is commonly thought. By not giving issues such as those discussed in this collection proper attention, either in the media or government, we may well be missing important opportunities to press effectively for improvements in the lives of many people as well as to affect overall East-West relations in a positive way.

To the extent that these countries are examined, they often are characterized solely by the ways in which they differ from each other, an approach that can lead to many misperceptions and distorted views. For example, popular images of Hungary — where store shelves are not empty, writers and artists have gained more latitude, citizens can travel abroad, believers have access to Bibles and other religious materials, and dissidents are not imprisoned and can even study in the West — dispute the more common image of a communist system, which is usually perceived to be closed to the outside world, facing chronic shortages, and subject to cruel and totally uncaring rule by an omnipresent state. Hungary often is viewed, therefore, as a unique and positive exception in the communist world.

Although Hungary may stand out in the degree of latitude granted its citizens, a fact that we fully acknowledge and welcome, the enclosed articles and essays reveal the important but often missed point that effective controls still exist, albeit in a more subtle and sophisticated form than blatant repression. In return for the positive developments that have taken place, Hungarian citizens must accept state-imposed limitations on their ability to act upon the same rights and freedoms that the Hungarian Government pledged fully to respect. If Hungarian citizens do not accept these limitations, as some of the authors of the works contained in this volume know well, the positive developments that have taken place suddenly can become fragile, arbitrary and treated by the Hungarian Government more as privileges to be granted or taken away than as fundamental rights to be protected.

The enclosed articles also show us that, regardless of whether repression is subtle or blatant, there will always be people who will challenge that repression by taking their government's promises seriously and acting upon their rights. Their writings deserve our attention, because, in acting upon their rights and defending the rights of others, in a very real sense they promote the larger goals of true security and cooperation in Europe as embodied in the Helsinki Final Act, which serve the interests of the peoples of all states involved.

Steny H. Hoyer
Co-Chairman

Alfonse M. D'Amato
Chairman

COMMISSION ON
SECURITY AND COOPERATION IN EUROPE
CONGRESS OF THE UNITED STATES

INTRODUCTION

The writings in this volume could not be legally published in Hungary today. They have been selected from illegal publications, sometimes called samizdat to emphasize the similarity to their Soviet namesakes, and sometimes identified as the "second public opinion," to distinguish them from official public opinion as represented by the state controlled mass communications media and publishing houses.

The mere existence of these publications indicates the limitations placed on free speech and public expression in what is so often dubbed the "most liberal" communist country by some Western observers. The absurd lengths to which the Hungarian government is willing to go to prevent the spread of uncontrolled information are best characterized in an interview with one of the publishers of these materials. In the course of describing how everything that was even vaguely connected with his activities was confiscated in his apartment during a police search, he mentioned that even his child's plastic printing toy, bought at a state owned shop, was taken away.

These publications exist in spite of the severe penalties which have been meted out to those who participate in their production and dissemination. Since Hungarian law requires that every duplicating machine, including the simplest mimeograph be registered, and since these machines are kept under lock and key at all offices, and since the law also prohibits the duplication of any material without some form of official permit, it is easy to prosecute those who prepare these publications. As a result, there have been many arrests, fines, and confiscations of property, especially in 1982 and in 1986.

Ironically, these repressive measures have not daunted the opponents of the regime. Some have been so often persecuted by the authorities and have been so totally excluded from society that they are no longer afraid of the police or the courts. Others, much younger than those in the previous group, have decided that they will not accept the limitations on personal freedom that are an inseperable part of life in the society created by the communists in Hungary. This latter group is possibly the most important, since there are indications that their numbers are growing.

The Hungarian authorities and their Soviet counterparts who are the ultimate guarantors of their power know that the number of those willing to challenge the system and its rulers is growing. One sign of their awareness has been the brutal suppression of a peaceful demonstration by more than a thousand young people on March 15, the anniversary of the the anti-Habsburg revolution of 1848. The ruthlessness of the police was particularly shocking since in recent years they have tolerated such spontaneous patriotic marches, carefully containing them, but keeping a civilized distance.

The authorities have also intensely tried to woo young people away from ideas that are antithetical to Marxist ideology, coupling these efforts with an unrestrained suppression of those who challenge the state's authority and the accepted ideology. The most interesting of those who suffer the consequnces of the latter actions are the adherents of fundamentalist and pacifist religious groups, particularly the Catholic followers of father Bulányi. Many people in their early twenties have chosen to serve 2 and 3 year terms in military prisons instead of performing active armed service, and the number of those who provide them moral and material support is increasing.

The list of those who are willing to challenge the state includes many more than the above. They range from the large group of environmentalists who signed protests against the building of a system of dams along the Danube between Gabcikovo (Bős) in Czechoslovakia and Nagymaros in Hungary, through large independent peace groups who were quickly and skillfully disbanded as a result of their lack of political sophistication, to small bands of working-class youth who were arrested and jailed for publicly singing rock songs which challenged the communist system and the Hungarian regime, and described the Soviet Union without using the usual sugar-coated cliches. And even these are only the cases about which some information has been gleaned in spite of the tight control that the Hungarian Socialist Workers [Communist] Party exerts over all communications media. Possibly the largest number of those who challenge the communist system are ordinary workers who in moments of unrestrained anger say things about communism, one of the leaders of the country or the Soviets, and thereby earn prison terms or fines.

This last group is the one Hungary's rulers fear the most, since they know that the ordinary people are the only ones who have the strength of numbers behind them and they all remember that in 1956, it was exactly these people who changed peaceful demonstrations by college students and intellectuals into a revolution.

Even though it is by now a cliche about totalitarian systems that they are most afraid of the free flow of information, the writings in this book are a reminder of the real meaning of that statement. Some of these are more desperate and dramatic than others, but they all attest to the desire of people to discuss their problems and complaints freely, no matter how brutal or how refined the oppression is under which they must live.

14

On this 30th anniversary of the 1956 Revolution, the appearance of a volume of writings which criticize conditions in Hungary is of particular significance. It shows that in spite of every effort by János Kádár and his cohorts, the spirit of 1956 has not died out. There are still men and women who are willing to challenge the injustices of the totalitarian system, even in its less brutal form. They want to point out that although oppression may not be practiced as overtly as it was under the Stalinist regime of Mátyás Rákosi, it exists nevertheless. It has been internalized by a whole nation which cannot hear or speak the truth, which cannot make any plans for its future but is forced to live in uncertainty from day to day. Instead of the firing squad or the hangman's noose, the average Hungarian faces the executioner in the form of heart attacks caused by overwork and stress in a country where many people work 80 or 100 hours a week to provide the basic amenities of life for their families. The rate of death for men between the ages of 35 and 49 is nearly double the European average. Those who do not face this executioner, often become their own. The suicide rate in Hungary was 46 per 100,000 in 1984, almost twice as high as that for Denmark, the country with the next highest rate.

As if that were not enough, Hungary's rates for alcoholism and divorce are also among the highest in the world. These figures and others have led many Hungarians to point out that the ugly reality of totalitarian oppression lives on under the gilded surface of Kádár's supposedly liberal communist state. Those who have dared to point this out are consciously acting in the spirit of the Revolution that Kádár helped suppress. There are different ideas about how this spirit may be revived 30 years after the bloody defeat of that idealistic fight for freedom. Some believe that reforms of the present system, if assiduously propagated will provide the most freedom that can be hoped for in the shadow of Soviet military might, while others insist that no such compromises should be made and that the ideas of freedom and independence that so many fought and died for in 1956 cannot be replaced by second-rate substitutes. Between these two extremes, there are a number of different programs and many groups who espouse them, but what they all have in common is the same desire to replace the present totalitarian system with one that is pluralistic and democratic, in the Western sense of that word.

* * *

SAMIZDAT IN HUNGARY

Based on a summary prepared by an editor of *Beszélő*

Samizdat existed in Hungary even in the early 1950's, despite unlimited state terrorism against any expression of dissent. The best Hungarian writers were reduced to silence, but nevertheless circulated their poems and novels among their friends and reliable colleagues. During this period, a great amount of illegal religious material was also distributed among followers of certain denominations. After the revolution in 1956, dozens of political manifestos, statements and essays were circulated among intellectuals, workers and students. If identified by the police, their authors served years in prison, as in the case of István Bibó, a member of the revolutionary government and an outstanding political thinker.

The Early Samizdat

The Russian word "samizdat" became familiar in the Hungarian language together with the Russian and Polish practices of uncensored publishing. Samizdat is a product of organized activities whose goal is to regularly edit and distribute uncensored literature. In Hungary, this activity, modelled on the Russian, and influenced directly by the Polish samizdat movement, began to flourish in 1977.

In the first four years, samizdats were simply duplicated by typewriters. They were carefully edited and sometimes they carried the trademark *Samizdat*. Because of the slow duplicating technique, the number of copies rarely exceeded one hundred. The copies were distributed by a network of volunteers or sold in the so called "Rajk Boutique", i.e., the private home of László Rajk, the son of the Communist Minister of the Interior in the post war Hungarian government who was executed after a show trial in 1949. The retail price of the copies just covered the costs of typing.

In this period, samizdat editors produced roughly 170 publications. The very first and one of the most important was called *Marxizmus a negyedik évtizedben* (Marxism in the fourth decade). In reply to the editor's (András Kovács's) question: "What does Marxism mean after the neo-Marxist hopes of the Roaring Sixties have collapsed?", the authors, predominantly former Marxists, described how they moved away from Marx. Another samizdat, the 800 page *Profil* (Profile), edited by János Kenedi, was a superb collection of poems, short stories, essays and studies, all of which had been rejected by official periodicals in the seventies with the explanation that they did not fit the "profile" of the magazine.

The most important early samizdat venture was the edition of the 1000 page *Bibó Emlékkönyv* (Bibo Memorial Book), edited by Ferenc Donáth and others, in honor of the above mentioned István Bibó. Bibó's analysis of Hungarian society and his theories about "principled compromise" are strikingly similar to KOR's (the Polish Worker's Defense Committee, the precursor of Solidarity) conception of limited revolution, an idea which strongly influenced Hungarian intellectuals. More than seventy highly established as well as dissident authors paid tribute to the late political thinker in this volume. The united group of intellectuals represented in the collection, alarmed the Party authorities so much that the Cultural Department of the Central Committee of the Hungarian Socialist Workers Party prepared a report on the collections and elaborated a plan for the "differential treatment" of its authors. The essence of this treatment was to divide the group by using a combination of threats, incentives, and misleading information. Although it was strictly confidential, the report was obtained by those sympathetic to the authors of the samizdat book, was smuggled to the West, was broadcast back to Hungary by *Radio Free Europe*, and was later published in samizdat.

In this period of typewriting, two magazines were also published. *Magyar Figyelő* (Hungarian Observer) concentrated on domestic affairs and on the fate of the Hungarian minority living in neighboring countries. *Kelet Európai Figyelő* (Eastern European Observer) included mainly translations from the samizdat and emigre literature of the Soviet bloc countries.

The "Gutenberg" Age of Samizdat

In 1981, influenced by the enormous independent press in Poland during the Solidarity period, various groups undertook the production of samizdat for larger circulation. The first mechanically duplicated piece was the fifth issue of the *Kelet Europai Figyelő*, published in August of 1981, under the special title *"A lengyel nyár"* (The Polish Summer). As a result of an unplanned coincidence, the next three duplicated samizdats reached their readers almost at the same time as the military takeover in Poland.

Jaruzelski's coup deeply shocked the nascent Hungarian opposition. Some felt their efforts were hopeless and resigned from active work on the basis of a critical review of the Polish experiment. Two of the early duplicated magazines, *Kisúgó* ("Out former", as opposed to Informer) and *Magyar Figyelő,* stopped publication. However, *Beszélő* (which literally means "Talker", but also refers to the permit given to prisoners to meet their visitors), a political quarterly, survived and *Kelet Európai Figyelő* was revived in 1985 as *Máshonnan Beszélő* (Talker from Elsewhere). *Beszélő* was signed by five editors: Miklós Haraszti, János Kis, Ferenc Kőszeg, Bálint Nagy and György Petri; *Máshonnan Beszélő* was signed by János Kenedi and János Kis. In December of 1981, the Hungarian minority group in Rumania started a periodical called *Ellenpontok* (Counterpoints). After the publication of its tenth issue in January of 1983, its editors were arrested and forced to put an end to their activities or to leave the country.

The first samizdat books were published by AB Independent Publishers in 1982. AB produced novels like *The Caseworker* and *The Loser* by György Konrád, *Animal Farm* by George Orwell, plays by Vaclav Havel and poems by György Petri. The publishers, Gábor Demszky and Jenő Nagy, edited several series of books including "Supplement to the History of Eastern Europe", "Poland", "Gulag" and "1956". In 1983, AB began its own monthly magazine called *AB Tájékoztató* (AB Information Bulletin). After a seven month publication hiatus, it was renamed *AB Hírmondó* (AB Messenger). Jenő Nagy later built up his own enterprise called the ABC Independent Publisher. Another publishing house, called Magyar Október (Hungarian October), is run by György Krassó. As its name indicates, M.O.'s program is to publish writings and documents from the Hungarian revolution in 1956. A team of artists called the "Inconnu Group" started their own publishing house called Arteria whose purpose was to publish works of "political art", documents of police persecution considered "objects," and an occasional news magazine, the *Inconnu Press.*

Such expressions of dissent are not limited to the democratic opposition. There are other independent groups like the Catholic basis communities whose many members reject armed service, peace activists who renounce the arms race, and the "Blues" (a Hungarian equivalent of the Western Greens) whose single campaign against the construction of a giant hydroelectric plant on the Danube was supported by thousands of citizens. These groups all produce samizdat. The Catholic communities traditionally distribute religious literature called "Christmas Presents", including documents of their polemic with the church hierarchy and information on judgments brought against conscientious objectors. The former peace group Dialogue published nine issues of its own typewritten news magazine, and the environmentalist Danube Circle publishes its duplicated *News*

Bulletin. Several independent artist groups also distribute uncensored materials.

By the end of 1985, several new magazines came into being; among them is *Demokrata* (Democrat), *Kronológia* (Chronology) and *Vakond* (Mole). In addition to the above mentioned book publishers, smaller publishers like Alulnézet (Perspectice from Below) Áramlat (Stream) or Szabadidő (Leisure Time) produced books, and some others were published without any publishing logos.

The selection of these pieces was subject to a number of limitations. First and foremost, there was little time to read the large volume of Hungarian samizdat material now available. There was not enough time to translate the newest writings, although some of these are particularly interesting since they present new, more radically democratic ideas than those found in earlier samizdat publications. There was only a limited amount of space, so that some interesting writings had to be abridged, while others could not be included. The limit on the number of editors and translators has led to a work that in spite of all our efforts is far from perfect.

Notwithstanding the above shortcomings, we feel that this is at least a partially representative sample of uncensored Hungarian writings. It should give the reader a general idea of what those who challenge the communist regime in Hungary find objectionable in it, and above all it should indicate the degree to which freedoms are denied to the average Hungarian.

WE ACCUSE

The New York Times, Nov. 5, 1956

We accuse the Soviet Government of murder. We accuse it of the foulest treachery and the basest deceit known to man. We accuse it of having committed so monstrous a crime against the Hungarian people yesterday that its infamy can never be forgiven or forgotten.

Lenin wrote in 1900: "The Czarist Government not only keeps our people in slavery but sends it to suppress other peoples rising against their slavery (as was done in 1849 when Russian troops put down the revolution in Hungary)." How apt these words sound today when we substitute "Soviet" for "Czarist," and 1956 for 1849.

Hatred and pity, mourning and admiration, these are our emotions today: hatred for the men and the system which did not hesitate to shed new rivers of innocent Hungarian blood to reimpose slavery: pity for the Soviet soldiers, duped into thinking they were fighting "Fascists" when they killed defenseless or nearly defenseless men, women and children; mourning and admiration for the heroic Hungarian people who feared not even death to strike for freedom.

Gone now are the last illusions. Moscow now stands self-exposed. The torrent of Soviet bullets yesterday did not kill only Hungary's freedom and Hungary's martyrs. Those bullets killed first of all the picture of a reformed, penitent Russia seeking to repudiate Stalinism and practice coexistence. Could Stalin have acted more barbarously than did his successors yesterday? Can we have any doubt now of what awaits us if we ever relax our vigilance and permit ourselves to become prey to Soviet might, as was Hungary yesterday?

The day of infamy is ended. The foul deed is done. The most heroic are dead. But the cause of freedom lives and is stronger than ever, nurtured by the blood of those who fell martyred in freedom's cause. The Hungarian people will never forget. We shall not forget. And out of hatred and tears is born the resolve to carry forward the struggle till freedom is triumphant.

HISTORY AND TRADITION

COMMEMORATION OF THE 1956 REVOLUTION AND ITS VICTIMS

An Interview with György Krassó

abridged from *Hírmondó 2, 1983*

Introduction

On 13 June 1983, after the last lecture preceding the summer recess of the Monday Free University (which consists of lectures in private apartments) the audience stayed on in the Gyula Lengyel Street apartment to listen to two commemorative lectures. In the first Gábor Demszky spoke about the East Berlin workers' revolt in 1953. Then György Krassó opened a program commemorating Imre Nagy, Pál Maléter, and Miklós Gimes (executed a quarter of a century ago, on 16 June 1958) and Géza Losonczy and József Szilágyi, who had been murdered earlier.

On the basis of his personal recollections, Krassó described the circumstances of the executions and the conditions under which the defendants of the Imre Nagy trial were kept in the last years and days of their lives.

Since we cannot reproduce the full text of this commemoration, we present an interview with György Krassó about his recollection of the events and his personal views about some of the questions discussed. In 1957, Krassó was sentenced to 10 years imprisonment.

On 12 February 1979 he was the first person to speak again at a public meeting about the events of 1956 as a democratic national revolution. In October 1981 in a private apartment he held a commemoration of the 25th anniversary of the revolution of 1956. He translated and edited Bill Lomax's well-known book "Hungary 1956."

Hírmondó: In your commemoration you described the life of the executed defendants of the Imre Nagy trial. Could you summarize briefly the content of your speech?

Krassó: I can say briefly that in 1958 Imre Nagy was 62 years old, and all the other defendants were 41 years old. All five defendants were communists. Imre Nagy had jointed the Bolsheviks as a Hungarian prisoner of war in Russia at the time of the Civil War, even before the Hungarian Communist Party had been founded. Losonczy and Szilágyi took part in the illegal activities of the Hungarian Communist Party during World War II. Pál Maléter and Miklós Gimes became communists at the end of the war. Imre Nagy was the Minister of Agriculture responsible for "redistributing" the lands (of large landholders, in 1945). Then he worked as a university professor. Later he was again minister and prime minister from July 1953 until April 1955, and then again from 24 October onwards. Losonczy and Gimes, after the war, were leading journalists at *Szabad Nép* (Free People), the Communist Party daily newspaper. Maléter was an officer on the Chief of Staff, in 1945, József Szilágyi was, one of the organizers of the new Hungarian police force in the provinces and later headed the personnel department of the Ministry of Home Affairs and then the security department of the Communist Party. Even though these facts are known, I wanted to recall who the people hanged after 1956 were, who were those who are still called counterrevolutionaries, restorers of capitalism and agents of the imperialists (in official history books).

H: But after all, they were not sentenced to death because of their activities in the party . . .

K: Of course not. There is another side to their lives. They were all communists by conviction and not because of career ambitions, so they soon found themselves in conflict with the party machine and sooner or later they had to realize the real nature of the political power they themselves were supporting. Already in 1930, at the Second Congress of the Hungarian Party of Communists, as the communist party was then called, which was held in the Soviet Union, Imre Nagy had been obliged to practice self-criticism for his "opportunist and rightist" views. In 1949, he opposed the Rákosi party leadership on aspects of its policy concerning the peasants. In 1955 he was expelled from the Communist Party, known as the Hungarian Workers' Party, and he was readmitted into the party only in October 1956. Losonczy was arrested in 1951 and was released only in 1954. Szilágyi was demoted in connection with the Rajk trial and then worked as a clerk and attended university evening classes. In 1954 Gimes was compelled to leave *Szabad Nép* and in 1955 was expelled from the party. All three were active opponents of Rákosi before the Revolution.

H: You have not said anything about Maléter . . .

K: As far as I know, before the outbreak of the Hungarian revolution, Maléter had had no contacts either with the party opposition or with any other opposition forces. In the higher ranks of the armed forces, Imre Nagy had few followers before 23 October 1956. In the following days he received more support, though not much. Pál Maléter was one of these recent supporters of Imre Nagy. As we heard from his widow at the commemoration of June 1953, in those days he told his wife that when the Germans had occupied the country he had fought against them, and he had welcomed the Soviets as liberators, but 12 years later he was no longer able to see them as liberators.

I would like to point out that the role of Pál Maléter will remain a much debated question. Gergely Pongrácz, the former commander of the Corvin Alley units, has violently attacked Maléter in his book which was recently published in America.

I would like to correct a mistake I made during the commemoration, when I said that Maléter was taken to the Soviet Union after his arrest. I had heard this version of events from a plain soldier who had been the driver of the negotiating team of the Hungarian side, and who had been taken to Ungvár, formerly part of Hungary, then of Czechoslovakia, now part of the Soviet Ukraine. I have since discovered that this soldier was mistaken, since Maléter was brought from Tököl to the KGB central command in Sashalom and subsequently to the Fő utca prison along with Sándor Kopácsi.

H: Let us go back to the members of the Imre Nagy group. Did they become the leaders of the revolution in October 1956?

K: It is difficult to answer this question unambiguously. The outbreak of the revolution was not planned or organized by anyone. With the exception of József Szilágyi, who on 22 October spoke in favor of the demonstration, all the other members of Imre Nagy's group were frightened of unpredictable consequences, even of the demonstration itself. Imre Nagy was already Prime Minister on the morning of 24 October, but even then he tried to dampen the popular movement. Even Gimes and Losonczy needed 3 or 4 days to reach the conclusion that they were witnessing a popular democratic uprising. What about Maléter? In the first days he was fighting against the insurgents in the Corvin Alley . . .

H: It almost sounds as if they were on the other side . . .

K: No, not at all, I am not saying that. The problem is more complicated. Look, I will tell you what my personal opinion is, and it is possible that I may hurt some people's feelings. The revisionists, i.e., the pro-Imre Nagy communists, were not at all revolutionaries, they were reformists. This is true both in relation to their objectives and to the means they used. They wanted to defeat the Rákosi-Gerő clique and its base of support. They wanted to improve the system, in an attractive, useful, democratic way, but they had not settled accounts with the main party dogmas. "We are the party," said Losonczy at the Petőfi circle, and the other members of the Imre Nagy group thought the same thing. They wanted more political liberty, but within the one-party system or at least within the framework of the system guaranteeing the leading role of the Communist Party. They wanted a more rational, more balanced economic policy and a significant rise in the standard of living, but always in the framework of the centralized planned economy. They would have reduced the dependence of Hungary on the Soviet Union but they would have maintained the country in the Soviet sphere of influence. By and large they were oriented towards Yugoslav Titoism. (Tito later betrayed them.) Furthermore, their methods were not revolutionary. They wanted to take the party under their leadership and what they were attacked for later is precisely what they did not do, they did not want to take any of the political problems to the streets. This attitude was motivated by tactics, ideology and interest . . .

A paradoxical situation came into being. When the revolution broke out, apart from the revisionist group, there was no other opposition organized in any sense. Such a thing could not have existed, since the ÁVH (State Security Authority) crushed all other attempts to organize an opposition. Not many people know that even in 1955 hangings were carried out, and what is more, for very minor political offenses. In any case, only the revisionists existed as a more or less organized political force. So in a few days they became the leading force of the revolution, at least at the governmental and political level.

Now, not all of this applied equally to Imre Nagy. He had always been more loyal to the party than his followers. He always respected party discipline, but on the other hand he was more farsighted than his followers were. It was very characteristic of him that when in 1955 he was excluded from power and was attacked in extremely violent terms, Imre Nagy addressed his self-defense and his memoranda to the Central Committee of the party. On the other hand, in these essays one can find ideas for a decentralized economy, for a multiparty system, for pluralism and, what is more, for neutrality. (See *On Communism in Defense of the New Course,* London, Thames and Hudson, 1957.) These two sides of Imre Nagy's personality emerged at the time of the revolution. In the first days, his loyalty to the party was dominant, but after 28 October, he whole-heartedly accepted the demands of the democratic national revolution, carrying them out to their ultimate and logical consequences. From that moment on, he did not abandon this position, even at the cost of his life.

*H:*And who do you think was right? The reformists, or those following the revolutionary tactics?

K: This question is timely, even now. The lesson of the Hungarian revolution was not analyzed anywhere in Eastern Europe, and even here in Hungary most people reached nothing more than the flat conclusions that "you must not bang your head against a brick wall," that is that the uprising was futile.

I have already said that nobody planned the revolution, it emerged as the logical consequence of events. Therefore those representing a revolutionary strategy did not exist before 23 October 1956. The reformists had good reason to believe that after the Soviet withdrawal from Austria in 1955 and after the 20th Congress of the Soviet Communist Party, it would have been possible to carry out a peaceful "destalinization," but there was no thought of bringing about changes by violent means.

I think it is important to point out that even if they had seen such a possibility, they would not have wanted a revolution. I believe the revisionists, who always spoke so much about the people, never believed in or trusted them. From their early youth they had been communists, and the communist movement had always had an elitist character. Even if the communists sometimes made use of the spontaneous actions of the masses, they always looked with suspicion at them. They were always afraid that these movements might take another direction, different from that constructed by the representatives of the so-called Revolutionary Theory. After several decades of party work in the communist movement, there could remain, and in fact there did remain, some well-intentioned reformers, but certainly no revolutionaries. On the other hand, the masses had reason to suspect that the reformist program was nothing more than a new manipulation, and even if Imre Nagy had taken the place of the former Stalinist leaders Rákosi and Gerő, in the end this would not have prevented things from slipping back on to the old track. This is why they did not put down their weapons even when, precisely as a direct consequence of their armed action, these changes had taken place. The example of Gomulka and the history of the last 15 years, the Czech reforms initiated from above and the fate of the Polish "self-limiting revolution", prove for me that the people were right.

H: Are you saying that any reformist attempt would have been mistaken?

K: No, a country cannot live in permanent revolution. This can happen only for a limited time. Comparatively peaceful and consolidated epochs are much longer, and it is during these periods that the advocates of sensible social and economic reforms can do most for the nation. As I see it, the problem is that in Eastern Europe the ruling powers cannot tolerate even the activities of reformists. Even in today's "liberal" Hungary only the advocates of (economic) reforms, and moreover, only the moderate ones among them, are allowed to speak.

Since radical revolutionary positions cannot be articulated publicly, a false legend has been created about reformists. In the long evolutionary periods they are unable to act really effectively. They are also unable to do so in a revolutionary situation, precisely because they have formerly criticized official policy and have been persecuted for this. Because of their notoriety and their partly organized existence, they actively play an influential role, which is then used for a reformist channeling of the people's radicalism. Now, this fact can have tragic consequences in revolutionary circumstances. In Eastern Europe this problem is always present.

But after all, in 1956, the Hungarians started a revolution. Was it ι̣ᴏᴛ precisely this which lead to the tragic consequences?

K: The Hungarian revolution has been the only movement in Eastern Europe which has reflected clearly and uncompromisingly what the common aspiration of these nations is, and the Hungarian movement has been the only one which has been able to win. Even if the external overwhelming forces could have suppressed it in blood, even if the whole world was to leave it unaided, even in its defeat it brought more results for the Hungarians than any other movement in this region. I think the best reform communists, and in the first place those executed at the Imre Nagy trial, acknowledged this fact at the end of October, and they put people before the party, were not willing to betray Hungary to foreign interests. This is why they had to die.

H: Are you saying that in the first days of November 1956 there came into being complete harmony between the insurgents and the government?

K: Apparently so. The government accepted all the most important demands of the uprising and in one of his radio speeches Imre Nagy especially emphasized the fact that the government acknowledged the local people's representative bodies created in the course of the revolution and would have based its actions on them. But the two aspects of the revisionists' policy I mentioned before were present also later on. The government did not consider its position sufficiently stable, and at the same time it believed the Soviet intervention to be avoidable only through diplomatic steps and through the fastest possible consolidation. It devoted most of its energy to this consolidation, neglecting in the meanwhile to prepare for the defense of the country. Left-wing students and intellectual organizations started an enormous propaganda campaign for the Imre Nagy government. The largest insurgent units were visited by pro-governmental agitators and cadets, apparently to teach them the use of arms. Béla Király, Sándor Kopácsi and Maléter created the Revolutionary Security Committee and the National Guard, and they wanted to disarm the insurgents who refused to join the pro-governmental organizations. Béla Király arrested Dudás (leader of a group called the Hungarian National Revolutionary Committee) and according to a declaration made by Király later, after he had emigrated, he would have guaranteed the respect of the government's authority by using arms if it became necessary. If Kopácsi is not exaggerating in his account, it would appear that an armed action was planned for 4 November for the arrest of many prominent personalities who did not recognize the authority of Imre Nagy. A great propaganda effort was made to stop the "senseless strike," and for starting work again on 5 November. Now, the "street" had had a policy different from that of the government, it considered the main threat to be a Soviet intervention and remained in arms.

H: But weren't all these steps you mention taken by the government and left-wing forces to avert the counterrevolutionary danger? Don't you think there was any such danger?

K: Inside the country there was no such danger. The Stalinists were in hiding, their leaders had fled abroad and former ÁVH men asked to be taken into protective custody. Who could have been threatening the revolution?

H: I did not make myself clear. I was thinking of forces which wanted to restore or to create a right-wing regime.

K: It is true, there were forces with such aspirations, but these forces were not counterrevolutionary. They were so called "right-wing" phenomena. A right-wing exists in every democratic country and it would have been very strange if these right-wing forces hadn't existed in Hungary, especially after the irrational and cruel Rákosi period, but the strength of the right-wing should not be overestimated. The bulk of the insurgents did not want any kind of restoration of capitalism, what is more, they wouldn't have allowed any such restoration to take place. Everywhere it was proclaimed from the rooftops that "the factories and the land will not be given back" and nobody said even in a whisper "let us give back the factories and land." On the political scene the leaders of the former governmental coalition parties declared their support for the Imre Nagy government. József Cardinal Mindszenty, the Roman Catholic Primate of Hungary, imprisoned in 1948 and released during the revolution, enjoyed great respect, but if he had really proclaimed a policy of restoration, he would have found very few followers.

H: What was the trial of Imre Nagy and his associates like and how did it proceed?

K: It was prepared in total secrecy. Even we had not heard anything about it in prison. Usually we knew about the cases being prepared. All the defendants were kept in the Fő utca prison. Géza Losonczy was murdered in December 1957. He was apparently killed on the 21st of that month, as he was being force-fed during a hunger strike.

The first day of the Imre Nagy trial was held under judge Zoltán Radó on 6 February 1958. It was, however, soon postponed with some specious excuse. It seems that at the time they had not yet decided the fate of the defendants. At the trial, but also during the interrogations, József Szilágyi spoke out so enthusiastically in favor of the revolution that his case was separated from that of the others and he was sentenced to death in April by Judge Vida. It is not known when and under what circumstances he was murdered but it is not likely that he was taken to the Gyűjtő, where death sentences were usually carried out. In the eventual official communique, the fact that his case had been separated from that of the others was not mentioned.

At the end of the next series of trials, which began on 9 June, the other members of the Imre Nagy group were sentenced on 15 June, a Sunday, by Judge Vida. It was not possible to appeal the sentence. There was no second trial. Appeals for pardons were turned down. Imre Nagy and Pál Maléter had refused to admit to any crimes, and Miklós Gimes acknowledged only his responsibility for what had happened during the revolution. Of the remaining eight defendants, five were sentenced to long periods of imprisonment (Sándor Kopácsi to life imprisonment; Ferenc Donáth to 12 years; Ferenc Jánosi to 8 years; Zoltán Tildy to 6 years and Miklós Vásárhelyi to 5 years). Imre Nagy, Pál Maléter and Miklós Gimes were sentenced to death. The death sentences were carried out the following day, the morning of 16 June. The public was informed of what had happened only a day later, on 17 June, in an official communique.

H: Is it known what Imre Nagy said when he availed himself of the right to say his last words?

K: What became known was what he did not say. The official press and the official white book on the case, (*The Counterrevolutionary Conspiracy of Imre Nagy and His Accomplices,* Budapest, Information Bureau of the Council of Ministers, 1958) obviously contained nothing on the subject, but almost every publication issued in the West contains the text of a dramatic declaration. According to this version, Imre Nagy, availing himself of the right to say his last words, said that he had twice tried to save the honor of socialism in the Danube valley but in both cases he had been prevented from doing so. He was now ready to give his life for his ideals and he was sure that sooner or later he would be exonerated and that three times as many people would come to his reburial as had gone to Rajk's in 1956 preceding the revolution. He was only afraid that his murderers would be among those commemorating him. A similar version of this last speech can also be found in Kopácsi's book *"In the Name of the Working Class".* Kopácsi was of course present at the trial, but even so it seems that these words were in fact never pronounced. According to a recollection which would seem to be more accurate, Imre Nagy did not avail himself of the right to say his last words. He said that the circumstances of the trial proved there was no point in saying anything. However, later, when the death sentence had been passed, and the judge, in accordance with the rules of judicial proceedings, asked him whether he wanted to appeal for pardon, he replied that he was not asking for it. He said he would be exonerated by the international labor movement. Now, taking into consideration the character of Imre Nagy, I think this version, so far unpublished, is more likely than the other one.

H: Aliz Halda also spoke about the trial at the June commemoration. What did she recall about these events?

K: The trial was held in such secrecy, Halda said, that even the defense lawyers had to sleep in the Fő utca prison complex. There was good reason for this, since this trial was unlawful in every respect, not only from the point of view of historical justice, since Imre Nagy's group had supported a cause with which all portions of the population had clearly sided, but it was also unlawful according to Hungarian laws in effect at the time. The government of Imre Nagy was a legitimate government. It was established according to the law. It was supported by the party and, what is more, by the Soviet Union. János Kádár was a member of this government, right until the end. Even after the kidnapping of Imre Nagy's group on 22 November 1956, Kádár stated that no legal action would be taken against them, "This is our promise and we will keep it." This is what Halda said. Indeed, this promise had been made through diplomatic channels, in verbal statements and in letters addressed to the Yugoslav Government.

H: Under what circumstances did the members of Imre Nagy's group live in prison? At the commemoration, you spoke about your personal recollections.

K: All of them were in the Fő utca, to be precise, the Gyorskocsi utca prison. After the trial, the surviving defendants were taken to the Gyűjtő on the outskirts of Budapest and then to the nearby town of Vác. I think their living conditions in prison were more or less similar to those of the other prisoners, only in the period immediately preceding the second part of the June continuation of the trial was their situation and their feeding slightly improved. At that stage they were taken to the writing rooms at the top floor of the prison. This technique of "amelioration for the trial" had also been used by the ÁVH at other times, like at the Rajk trial.

H: And how did the other prisoners live in the Fő utca prison? Were you there at the time?

K: Yes. I was arrested on 15 November 1956, and 3 days later, having been first taken to the 5th District and then to the general Soviet Command, I was brought to Fő utca. At the time, Maléter and Kopácsi also must have been there, but I didn't know Kopácsi then. The prison was in the hands of the Russians. The interrogations were conducted by KGB officials through interpreters. The minutes of these interrogations were subsequently taken to the Soviet Union. In any case they were unavailable for the later judicial proceedings. All of this shows quite clearly what the reality of the situation was, who those really wielding power in the country were.

I must say that the Soviet treatment was more human than the later Hungarian one. It is true that the living conditions were quite primitive. It was for example impossible to receive items for personal hygiene, relatives were not even informed of our whereabouts. So, instead of toilet paper we used the pages of the mainly Soviet books of the prison library. There was no possibility for washing or changing our underclothes, and so forth, but the Soviet interrogation officer, a KGB lieutenant colonel, did not beat me. At most he looked at me threateningly. The Russian guards, simple soldiers of the KGB, were friendly and often gave us mahorka tobacco and a piece of Pravda to roll it in. A cell usually contained two prisoners. In the daytime we could do almost anything, even sleep. We were able to speak with the prisoners of the adjacent cells through the walls. Sometimes the noise was very loud, for example the women in the prison began to sing. On such occasions the guards used to walk up and down shouting, "Tisha, tisha," in Russian meaning "quiet, quiet," which sounds in Hungarian like "wow!"

We were "taken over" by the Hungarian political police at the beginning of January, at least on the floor where I was held. We found out one morning when we heard the kick on the door and the abuse in Hungarian. We were forbidden to lie in our beds, to speak loudly, and our beds had to be made as in the military, with covers taut and square. For that matter this bed-making mania, derived from the best Habsburg traditions, followed us for the rest of our prison days. With the Hungarians, our personal hygiene improved, we were shaved once a week, we received soap and toilet paper, but seldom any books. We were sometimes even given clean underclothes, but our treatment was much rougher. The guards' shouts and abuse became a permanent feature of our lives and sometimes prisoners were beaten up. Later this set-up was changed. We were moved to solitary cells and deadly silence replaced the shouting. Previously it had been dark at night, and we had been allowed to sleep whenever we wanted to. Now instead, day and night, we had a very strong light burning above the cell door, and during the night it shined right into our eyes, because we were allowed to sleep only in a strictly defined way. We had to face the grated and opaque double-glass window opposite the door, and had to lie on our backs and keep our arms over the blanket. Of course this way most of us could not sleep and even if we managed to do so, we turned in our sleep, so the guards kept kicking the cell door throughout the night to wake us. During the day we were exhausted, but were strictly forbidden to lie down. This was a cynical way of trying to break a person's will. It was cynical since the male nurse who came to see us daily was willing to give us sleeping pills upon request. This way the situation was aggravated since we couldn't sleep anyway, so we were even more exhausted during the day.

The isolation was part of the psychological treatment. We were not allowed to keep anything in our cells. Even the washbasin, a pail of water and a broomstick were made available only for a few minutes a day. It was impossible to speak to anyone. The guards gave us mess-tins, bread and water through the cell shutter, without saying a word. They only asked us every evening, "Doctor or interrogation?" Even if we asked for one of them, regardless of which one, weeks or months passed without any hearings or examinations. The point of this treatment was to make us want these meetings and to see the possibility of having them as somehow redeeming us of our miseries. The silence, the inactivity and solitude almost drove prisoners with weaker nerves insane. We began to see the whole world in an unreal way.

Sometimes a cellmate was taken away for a few days, but then it almost always turned out that he was an informer who went from one cell to another to do his work.

It was in April 1957 that I was taken from the Fő utca prison, but half a year later, in October 1957, I was returned there from Mária-nosztra, near the Czechoslovak border. I had been sentenced without appeal to 10 years prison, but the investigations into the Mérei case continued. So I spent another 3 months at Fő utca. The living conditions were the same, but now, maybe since I had been in the continuously buzzing and "event-filled" Markó prison, at the pretrial prisons of Budapest, Gyűjtő and Márianosztra, the inhuman silence, the solitude and the sterile oppression of Fő utca was even more frightening. From time to time I heard the prisoners' cries. I may even have heard Géza Losonczy. I was questioned only on the first day. Then 3 months later, in January 1958, without a word from the interrogator, I was taken away. It is probable that this was the time when the whole political investigative apparatus had been switched to the preparation of the Imre Nagy trial, and the other cases were temporarily put aside. In fact I heard that Captain Virág, who had questioned me in October, had become the interrogator of Pál Lőcsei, a revisionist journalist, formerly with *Szabad Nép*. Lőcsei, a close friend of Gimes, was finally sentenced separately. He was not among the defendants of the Imre Nagy trial because he had refused to give evidence against his companions.

H: Do you mean to say that the choice and role of the defendants had not been fully predetermined?

K: Of course not. One should remember the Rajk case in which for example Béla Szász was excluded for similar reasons. The defendants and the charges were always changed according to the political needs of the time. In these 1957 trials, take for example the Fősi-Angyal case, the Géza Pécs-Szirmai and Fátyol-Cselik cases. Before any sentence was passed, they extracted the case of István Angyal from the first, Ottó Szirmai from the second, and Ferenc Cselik from the third, putting them together with other defendants, and then initiating separate proceedings for the new group. Many points were taken into consideration. For example, in one case, only a limited number of defendants could be hanged. Of the above six, three were executed. I also started out in a case originally devised for at least five defendants, one of whom was László Gyurkó. But in the end I remained alone. I was made into an organization by myself, and Gyurkó became a witness for the prosecution. The purpose in this case was to differentiate the sentencing. Gyurkó was also sentenced, but he got a few months on probation for agitation, while I got 10 years for conspiring against the system. Willingness to cooperate with the investigating authorities was important. I am not exaggerating if I say that on the basis of one's reaction one could be hung but one could also end up a member of parliament or a prime minister. [Gyurkó had in fact subsequently a flourishing literary and political career as a writer, theatre director and member of parliament. He has recently written an official biography of János Kádár, Ed.]

H: Were a variety of options also taken into consideration for the Imre Nagy trial?

K: Of course. In the first place, even at the beginning of March 1957 only a Maléter-Kopácsi trial had been planned. Finally, they were given a written indictment which referred to their mutinous behavior as military and police officers, but this was soon withdrawn. The preparation for and the convening of the trial may have had something to do with the hysteria about the "MUK" slogans in March 1957. MUK stood for "Márciusban újra kezdjük" ("In March We Start Again"), an opposition slogan at the time, similar to the 1982 Polish one "the winter is yours, the spring will be ours."

It seems certain that at that time not even the outlines of the Imre Nagy trial had been defined. The majority of the defendants of the 1958 trial were enjoying Romanian "hospitality," during which Imre Nagy was also offered a ministerial position if he practiced self-criticism. At the time, Zoltán Tildy was still free, and living in his Budapest flat. Between the Spring of 1957 and June 1958, after the idea of the conspiracy-treason-revolution started to take shape, statements based on this fabrication were made more and more frequently. But even at this stage, the plans were changed several times.

According to Kopácsi's memoirs, there was a period in which Béla Király, who had emigrated to the West, would have been included among the defendants. Then Géza Losonczy was no longer suited to the role which had been assigned to him at the trial since his mental condition had deteriorated as a result of the conditions of life at the

Fő utca prison. He was eliminated from the list of defendants by his death. There was a change of policy in February 1958. This was the unannounced separation of the case of József Szilágyi. The actual selection of the defendants on a political basis is acknowledged by the white book issued later about the trial. It tries to explain why there was no judicial process against György Lukács, Júlia Rajk, Szilárd Újhelyi, Zoltán Vas and others, despite the fact that this group included people "who had harmed the Hungarian people with their activities." There was an important change in the formulation of the charges and in the motives behind the sentencing at the final trial, in the sense that connections with Yugoslavia stood out as the main offenses against the state.

H: So you see the final form of the trial as having foreign policy implications.

K: In part only. The Soviet propaganda campaign against Yugoslavia started in the Spring of 1958 and the gesture towards China undoubtedly played its part. However, I believe the significance of these things is often overestimated. The Stalinists in the party under the leadership of Révai [former Stalinist leader who died in 1959, Ed.] had demanded from the very beginning the incrimination of the revisionists, and the official declarations also became more and more threatening. The purpose of the trial, prepared under the direction of the Soviet KGB colonel Sumilin, was to prevent any further dissolution inside the Soviet bloc. They wanted to show both to the Hungarians and the other East European nations that they would not tolerate a weakening of party control nor changing the relationship to the Soviet Union even according to the ideas of the "revisionists" or the adherents of a "popular front." It is probable that this is why in the end Tildy had to be taken along with the revisionists. [Tildy had been the leader of a post-war government coalition party, Ed.]

They achieved their purpose. For 10 years, until 1968, a dead silence descended over East Europe. Hungary sank into political apathy. Even after more than a quarter of a century, opposition groups see the 1956 option, the option of a national revolution, as hopeless. To achieve this end, not only was the trial of Imre Nagy necessary, but also several hundreds, possibly thousands, of hangings, the imprisonment and internment of tens of thousands and the intimidation of millions.

H: In your opinion, who made the decision about the death sentence?

K: The decision was probably made in Moscow, on Sumilin's advice.

H: Manypeople think that János Kádár could have prevented the execution of Imre Nagy.

K: Nobody can be certain about this, perhaps not even he knows. It is, however, certain that both the leaders of the Soviet party and the

Hungarian Stalinists exerted strong pressure on Kádár. Even if the final decision was made in the Kremlin, the possibility of bargaining for the lives of the defendants still remained. Kopácsi says that his life was also bargained for on the telephone with Khrushchev. In my opinion, at the time Kádár was already indispensable to the Soviets, so his resignation could hardly have come into consideration. There had already been a Hungarian prime minister who committed suicide rather than break his word. [Pál Teleki, who committed suicide in 1941 rather than break the non-aggression pact he had signed in 1940 with Yugoslavia, Ed.]

There is no sign, however, that Kádár even threatened to resign or that he ever took any other step to prevent the political murders. Because the question concerns not only the case of the Imre Nagy group, but also that of possibly thousands of people. Furthermore, the death sentences carried out on a conveyor belt were not handed down from Moscow. The Kádár speeches before and after the Imre Nagy trial were in line with the bulk of the statements authorizing these sentences. I am not saying that János Kádár was happy with all these cruel events, but it remains a fact that with the execution of Imre Nagy he got rid of his most dangerous rival, the man who could have taken his place in a later period of consolidation, conciliating the government and the nation.

H: How were the executions actually carried out?

K: I have already referred to the fact that in January 1958, I was taken from the Fő utca prison to the Gyűjtő prison. Here, at the end of March, I was moved to the ground floor of the Kisfogház, a small jail inside the Gyűjtő complex near the cells of those sentenced to death. The reason for this transfer could have been that the above mentioned investigations were being continued even then coupled with an attempt to isolate me and break my will. I lived for 5 months among those sentenced to death, more accurately in one of the cells adjacent to them.

At the time, there were 40 or 50 prisoners there. Their number was more or less stable, despite the fact that executions were being carried out continuously. There were mornings on which several people were hanged, one after another. New prisoners sentenced to death were a regular feature of prison life. In the majority of cases, these prisoners had been sentenced in the first round of trials. There was, therefore, the possibility of a reprieve for them as a consequence of a changed sentence in the second round, or if they had received a pardon subsequently. But there were very few cases in which this happened. On the contrary, the second round of sentences were usually harsher than the first.

Those executed in the morning, usually had to be examined by a doctor on the previous day. I do not know of any case in which Doctor Szabó, the commander of the prison hospital, an otherwise benevolent dentist, certified anybody as being in a state of health unsuitable for execution. The prisoner was first shaved, put in chains to prevent him from committing some "irremediable act," i.e., suicide, and was taken for the night to an empty cell. He was allowed to write letters but it appears that these letters were in fact never delivered.

The executions were always carried out by hanging, at approximately 6 a.m. in the court of the Kisfogház near the building wall. We always knew that there would be one execution or more when we heard hammering at dawn. The gallows were wedged in those 4 or 5 square-shaped openings which were normally covered by iron plates. On such occasions, the guards delayed waking us up, bringing us water and breakfast. They walked silently in felt slippers, kept looking through the peep holes of the cell doors, to see if there was any suspicious activity or movement. We heard the trampling of feet, the doors being flung open, the clinging of chains and the prisoner being taken out shouting his name for the last time and saying farewell to a former cellmate and almost always invoking freedom or Hungarian independence.

Some people wept, some had to be dragged, some still tried to prove their innocence, some called out to their companions to prove their innocence or to avenge them, and some struggled with the executioners.

The hangman was Major Kovács and one of his assistants was Sergeant-Major Karácsony.

Then we heard those undescribable but characteristic noises from the court: trampling, jostling, rattling, some official text being read out and the loud or faltering last words of the accused. Almost without exception these words were about the revolution, Hungarian liberty and independence. Soon afterwards normal life in the prison resumed. The cell door was opened and the guards entered, and standing at attention we had to report, "Mr. Warden, I respectfully report that the number of detainees in this cell is 2. No abnormal events occurred during the night."

It was known that the man sentenced to death was made to stand on a stool. The rope was fastened both to his hands and tied behind his back and around his neck. The stool was pushed out from under him and his neck was broken by the pull of the rope and the twist of the head.

The moment of death was certified by the prison doctor, Doctor Szabó. The body or bodies were taken for a short time to a place reserved for this purpose, and were then taken in the morning hours to section 301 of the Rákoskeresztúr cemetery facing the prison. They were put into unmarked pits there.

Imre Nagy, Miklós Gimes and Pál Maléter were probably executed under similar circumstances. The executioner, Major Kovács, called in sick that day and Sergeant-Major Karácsony took his place.

H: Were you still at the Kisfogház when Imre Nagy and his companions were executed?

K: No. All of us, including those who had been sentenced to death, were transfered during the last days of May or the first days of June to the ground floor of "Right 2," that is the Second Department of the Right Star section of the main building of the Budapest National Prison (Gyűjtő). We had not understood anything about the reason for these changes. We took the fact that until the beginning of June there were no executions as a promising sign. At the time, we did not know that they were preparing a place for the Imre Nagy group in the Kisfogház. Now, on the morning of 16 June, we in the "Right Star", far from the Kisfogház, saw the well-known signs I had described above. By the afternoon we knew that Imre Nagy and two others had been hanged. We discovered the identity of the others only later.

The majority of prisoners had little or no sympathy for communists, but the execution of Imre Nagy was a shocking event for all of us. He symbolized the revolution. Hungarian liberty and independence went to the grave with him.

H: The lead article of the 1983 first number of *Irodalmi Újság,* now published in Paris, describes the circumstances of the execution. Is that account accurate?

K: There are some mistakes in it. I do not know of any case in which a gas mask was forced on the head of those who were to be executed as this account alleges happened with Imre Nagy. The bodies were not taken to the cemetery in the evening and not on a cart with rubber-tires but in the morning on a creaking one.

The author of this account seems to think that "a closed, completely sound-proof small enclosure without windows" was built around the gallows even before June 1958. This enclosure was built only after the execution of Imre Nagy, probably to prevent any sounds being heard and photos being taken. Here I want to point out that the memoirs of Sándor Kopácsi also give a false or unlikely version of the events. It is not true, as he says, that in the cemetery there are numbers on the graves. I also think it unlikely that János Kádár would have been present at the execution of Imre Nagy. I do not believe Kopácsi's statements to the effect that Kádár and other leading functionaries had to listen to the Imre Nagy trial from the beginning to the end in a room adjacent to the courtroom. How could Kopácsi have known that this was so?

H: What was the international reaction to the Imre Nagy trial? Have you heard anything about it?

K: I have read in the book *The Truth About the Imre Nagy Affair,* published in the West, that the Italian Socialist Nenni gave back his Stalin prize and Marcello Venturi, an editor of *L'Unita* (the newspaper of the Italian Communist Party) resigned the same night. Nehru was shocked and protested against the "cruel and base procedure." Krisna Menon, Mendes-France, Camus, Sartre's review Les Temps Modernes and writers, artists and public personalities in every part of the world also protested. The Western Communist parties lost many members, just as they had after 4 November 1956. In Hungary there was silence. I do not know of anybody who even tried to raise his voice. What about the intelligentsia? Ten months earlier almost all prominent Hungarian writers, more than 250, were successfully pressured into signing a memorandum to the United Nations, in which they proclaimed their confidence in the Kádár government and in which they said that the Soviet military intervention was justified.

H: Was the Imre Nagy trial the beginning of the repression or the end of it?

K: Neither. The repression, the executions and the heavy prison sentences, started at the end of 1956 and lasted for 3 years, until 1 January 1960, even though there were some executions in 1960, and even in 1961, in cases having to do with 1956. The Imre Nagy trial came during the period of harshest repression and revenge.

H: Now a last question. How was the commemoration of 13 June prepared? Did you know in advance that *Radio Free Europe* would broadcast it on one of its programs? And have you suffered any retaliations because of this?

K: Very briefly:

1. This commemoration would have been appropriate even years and decades ago, but we made the decision to hold it that morning, which is why it was so improvised.

2. I did not know that *Radio Free Europe* would broadcast it, and I would certainly have preferred if *Radio Kossuth* (First [Official] Hungarian Program) had transmitted it.

3. I was summoned at the beginning of August to the Passport Department of the Ministry of Home Affairs and two police officers told me that my passport request, both for a western and an eastern one, had been refused because I had committed this "act." I have never in my life had a western passport (i.e. passport for traveling in western countries) and the "red" one (i.e., a passport for traveling in Soviet bloc countries) was also taken from me several times, the last time in 1981. So the official explanation did not seem quite persuasive.

H: I have one last question. Hungarian emigre circles have asked the

Hungarian Government to reveal the whereabouts of the graves of those executed. What is your opinion about this step? And do you think the Hungarian Government could rehabilitate Imre Nagy and his co-defendants?

K: I am in full agreement with this initiative. Decency and compassion demand, what is more, our laws forbidding the violation of the memory of the dead prescribe, that the graves should be identified by name, and that the identity of those in them must be revealed. But I do not think that without widespread internal social pressure, the Hungarian authorities will consent. As far as I know, even the latest requests of the relatives of those executed were refused a few months ago. There are many reasons for this refusal, not the least of which is the fact that an acceptance of these requests could start a chain reaction and the identity and number of those executed 25 years ago would be disclosed. That is a large number. I consider even more unlikely the exoneration of those executed. The people who were responsible for and allowed the repression at the time are still in power. I believe the destiny of section 301 and the cemetery can be changed only by the Hungarian nation itself.

YOUTHS GATHER TO COMMEMORATE
1956 REVOLUTION

Beszélő 11, 1984

Candles burn every year on 1 November at the entrance to the Farkasrét Cemetery. Officially, they say that the candles are lit for those missing or deceased abroad. The popular belief in Pest is that they are lit for the casualties of the revolution. This year, an unusually great number of youths gathered around the few square meters of flower bed near the entrance. Whether they were thinking of the revolution or of Father Popielusko, the Polish priest murdered a few days earlier, or of their own deceased friends — no one knows. In any case, the police standing about the gate eyed them nervously.

Many of the 1956 generation have commemorated the day of the revolution every year for nearly three decades now. Some say today that for those who celebrate 23 October the revolution is history. Most recently, some young workers gave us an account of their small commemoration. All those present were younger than twenty. The first was a bodyshop worker, the second an automobile driver, the third an occasional worker, the fourth a shoemaker trainee, and the youngest, the only girl, age 17, a seamstress trainee. This is their letter, which was delivered to our editors, in its entirety:

23 October 1984, Tuesday

"We wish a blessed holiday to all our dear listeners," the radio crackles on the 31m shortwave band. The apartment is decorated with flags and ribbons. Of all our friends notified almost at the last minute, five have gathered at 6 o'clock in the evening. A holiday speech opens the program. Applause. A political joke heard on Radio Free Europe lightens the mood. Then a girl presents a section of the preface to Bill Lomax's "Hungary, 1956." A brief discussion follows: although the following song actually relates to the Prague Spring, it reflects the spirit of the revolution. And now the record is already spinning: Illés' "March, 1848." Two of us read Bibó's "Proclamation to the Nation." Numb Silence . . . From the cassette "Voice of the

Revolution" we hear György Petri's poem and Illés' "If I Were a Rose." "And if the tank should one day tread on us . . ." everyone joins in. Then we stand up and chant the strains of the national anthem. We chat a little longer, and go our separate ways. The next day some friends express their regrets that they heard of the event too late, or not at all. They seem sincere. It doesn't matter — next year October will come again, and so will the holiday. With this ceremony we young people also give notice to the stonemasons of this crumbling dictatorship, that "WE WILL NOT FORGET!"

PUBLIC REPORT ON POLITICAL PERSECUTIONS OF 1945-56 DEMANDED

Hírmondó 1, 1985

The Argentine weekly *El Periodista* published a complete list of the names of the 1351 persons accused by the so-called Sabato report of violating human rights in the course of fighting against the leftist Montonero-terrorists at the time of the military dictatorship in the seventies. Writer Ernesto Sabato, as president of the nationwide committee dealing with the affairs of missing persons, handed the report to the president of the state, but the government published it only in a brief summary and omitted the list of names. This is the gap filled by *El Periodista*.

In connection with this news item, we would like to know, has a comprehensive and exhaustive report on the unlawful actions which violated human rights and were perpetrated by the authorities between 1945-56 in Hungary ever been prepared, or has a list of the names of those who carried out these actions been compiled? Was there ever at least a list of the henchmen of the Recsk internment camp? What newspaper could publish such a list of names, even today, 30 to 40 years after the events?

We would like to indicate our outrage.

Another news item, also from November of last year. The Chilean government declared a state of emergency, on the basis of which searches were carried out at the offices of two oppositionist organizations — the Democratic Popular Movement and the Socialist Block. It is illegal to hold meetings without advance permission. Advance press censorship was introduced and six oppositionist periodicals were banned.

We do not have the least bit of friendly feeling toward Pinochet's dictatorship, yet we still want to ask in connection with this news item: What do you get out of this bit of news? We learn from this that, before the state of emergency was declared, there existed in Chile oppositionist parties and they were even allowed to function freely and oppositionist periodicals were published. Incidentally, we have known this all along.

And if we become upset because of the temporary narrowing of political rights, we cannot become upset for the same reason in Hungary's case, because in our country these rights have not been temporarily limited but summarily liquidated.

HUMAN RIGHTS ABUSES

THE INTERNAL EXILE OF LAJOS NAGY

Abridged from an article by György Krassó

Beszélő 15, 1985

People mistakenly think that only under (the Stalinist Regime of Mátyás) Rákosi has internal exile been used as a punishment against the "enemies of the regime."

A glaring current example of internal exile is the case of Lajos Nagy, who turned 60 in January 1985. On 15 February 1983, he was released from prison after 31 years (with two short interruptions in 1956 and 1976), which were the result of five different judicial proceedings against him. His first conviction of 12 years was for "food profiteering," while the others were principally for "political crimes." Finally, in the 70's, he was convicted of taking part in a "counterrevolutionary conspiracy" in prison.

The day Lajos Nagy was released, he was told to report to the Budapest police station in District XIX, where he had last lived. Contrary to his expectations, he was not given a personal identity card. Instead, he was read an order saying that he was being put under police surveillance and was being sent 250 km from Budapest to a place near the Romanian border, where he had been assigned a small dwelling which he was required to inhabit.

The order was valid for one year, and was renewable three times for a year at a time. According to changes in the law since then, a sentence of internal exile now starts with three years, which can later be extended. The justification for the order was that Lajos Nagy had manifested "antisocial tendencies" and lacked a job or a place to live in Budapest, so that nothing tied him to the city. Nagy said that although his former apartment had been torn down, he did have a place to live in Budapest and wanted to get a job there immediately. The only reason he did not register his address and get a job was that he had not received a personal identity card. He had ties in Budapest, because his sister lived there.

In spite of the above, his appeal was rejected within 24 hours by the central police authority of Budapest without considering the facts he had presented, and leaving him no recourse to other legal remedies. Only then did he receive his personal identity card, on which his place of exile had been entered as his address. He had eight days to move to the village of Kutas, in the Komád district. There he was assigned to work at the Biharkeresztes State Farm, with wages of 1600 forints per month. The officially established essential minimum in 1983 for a single person was 2130 forints.

Lajos Nagy's situation was made worse by another fact. While he was in prison, he had divorced his wife, and without his knowledge, the authorities had put his minor daughter up for adoption. The identity of the adoptive parents was unknown to him.

Despite repeated oral and written requests, Lajos Nagy was never given permission to go to Budapest, although he had, among others, medical reasons for wanting to go there. During the first year of his exile, he was sentenced to 40 days in jail because on one occasion he left his assigned settlement without permission. In February 1984 his exile was extended by a year, on the grounds that he had violated the terms of the police surveillance order. Following this extension Nagy was especially careful not to violate any rules, and was commended by the managers of the state farm for his work. Nevertheless, in February 1985 his exile was extended for another year, with the explanation that his "ability to work had deteriorated."

By this time Nagy was in the Berettyóújfalu Hospital. According to the law in effect, a sick person needing medical care could not be subjected to enforced exile, so that the order against Nagy should have been terminated. Since then, the law has been modified, (r/1985/VII.20.B.M.) and now there is no legal obstacle to keeping a sick person in exile. When Nagy becomes more incapacitated, he will be placed in a state home for the old, even though he has a relative in Budapest who is willing to take care of him.

(Shortly after the publication of the above article, Lajos Nagy died in internal exile at the age of 60).

BACKGROUND AND MOTIVATION OF
570 'POLITICAL OFFENDERS'

Hírmondó 5, 1984

We presented statistics on political prisoners and prisoners of conscience in our first issue. We pointed out that in the past 20 years, the overwhelming majority of political prisoners went to jail on charges of agitation. Based on data from various sources, it was also shown that since 1965 about 5,700 political crimes have taken place in Hungary. According to an analysis of the crime figures, intellectuals are blatantly underrepresented among political offenders. Those with only low-level schooling show up all the more often on the lists of repressive justice as victims.

An article appeared in *Magyar Jog* (Hungarian Law) which deserves attention. The editors and printers were so surprised, that they could not even print the title correctly. The article, written by Dr. Lajos Kovács, an instructor at the Academy for Police Officers, was entitled "Empirical Reasons Behind Offending Authority and Community." But if you read it you realize that the real title should be "Agitation and Offending the Community, etc." (igazgatás = administration/ authority; izgatás = agitation.)

In the course of the empirical study mentioned in the title of the article, the writer analyzed 402 cases involving 570 suspects. As he said on page 127, "the majority of criminal proceedings of the past 10 years." He discusses agitation and offending the public interest simultaneously, since the Criminal Code has redefined agitations as an offense against the public interest, as of 1 July 1979.

Dr. Kovács differentiates between the reasons for and the circumstances of crimes. The following is his system:

Direct Motives	Cases	Percent
Inimical stance	110	19.3
Enemy of the Public Good	126	22.1
Enemy Propaganda	98	17.2
Influence of Friends and Family	18	3.2
"Existential Reasons"	4	.7
Real or Alleged Reasons	97	17.0
Alcohol	236	41.4

Direct Motives	Cases	Percent
Chronic Mental Illness	56	9.8
Lack of Intelligence	155	27.2
Other	39	6.8
	1,050	*

*Note: One individual may have had more than one motive.

We calculated the percentages based on the total of 570 accused. The officially recognized motivations clearly show what the police and criminal investigations regard as reasons for "agitation" and offending the community. The percentage of those in the "lack of intelligence" category is noteworthy. We will provide more data about this. The "chronic mental illness" category is also without explanation. We are aware of the use of psychiatry in criminal investigations. Take, for example, the case of Pakh. Luckily, it is used a lot less here than in the Soviet Union. We cannot be sure that those who made the offending statements were mental patients. If they were mentally ill, then why didn't the authorities apply the laws pertaining to them? It must be pointed out that the criminal code excludes anyone who is mentally ill from prosecution and punishment.

The goals of the "actions" could not be determined in 205 cases. "Where they could be determined, the following reasons appear: desire for recognition, spreading of views, protest against administrative actions, revenge, 'criticism,' forbidden border crossings, attempts to be rewarded for their actions, threats because of alleged grievances, desire to go to another correctional institution or back to prison, organization of a conspiracy, draft dodging, 'only' intending to insult, promoting broadcasts of RFE (Radio Free Europe), spreading information about the superiority of Hungary. The list goes on and on. In some cases since 1980, the intent was to bring attention to the events in Poland." (p. 128)

A lot can be learned from this list. For example, anyone who protests a police action had better choose his words carefully, because they may convict him of agitation. For many unlucky individuals, being in prison is better than being "free." Some who try to make their youthful dreams reality by avoiding military service are put in jail and accused of not agreeing with government national policy. But one can get into jail by simply refusing to comply with the draft law.

The reference to Poland indicates that Hungarian workers did not take such a clear stance against strikes as domestic propaganda had proclaimed. However, criminal investigations did everything in their power to silence these sympathetic voices. Therefore, this warns us of the fact that in Hungary, if one expresses an opinion deviating from the official line about other socialist nations, then this is called agitation.

It would be good to know, what an instructor at the Academy for Police Officers meant by saying "the acts were sometimes surreptitious." (p. 128) The average reader is forced to conclude that one does not always have to actually do something, since it will suffice if the police think that a crime has been committed . . . In three-quarters of the cases, however, the "act was committed openly." The "perpetrators" alluded to: the correction of mistakes, the freedom to criticize, the defense of democracy, defense of the rights of workers, freedom to propagate religious views, the correct interpretation of historical facts, opposition to war, etc., (p. 128) Just think, what a long list of things can be called incitement in Hungary . . .

The evaluation of family situations is a complex problem. What are we to think of the assertion that step-parents instill a greater tendency to rebellion than natural parents? Or, what about the fact that state-run foster homes turn people against the state more than private ones? Indeed, if the writer were to draw a sociological conclusion, concluding that a disadvantaged background, poverty and cultural alienation are the main motivations behind "incitement" and "anti-state" statements, then he would call attention to the suppression of social discontent by the criminal justice system. However, the indicators for social background show, without requiring additional comment, that in most of the cases involving incitement, expressions of emotion by those at the lowest levels of society, the uneducated, and the have-nots appear as criminal offenses.

Education Level of Suspects

	People	Percent
Illiterate	5	.9
1-4 grades	29	5.9
5-8 grades	389	65.8
Interrupted High School	29	5.9
High School	70	12.3
Some College	21	3.7
Completed Higher Education	27*	4.7*

* The writer lists seven categories, but only gives six sets of numbers. We calculated the last one, so the total would be 570.

Cultural-Intellectual Level

	Cases	Percent
Primitive	156	27.4
Average	223	39.1
Good	75	13.2
Can Be Called High	24	4.2
Indeterminate	92	16.1

So, three-quarters of the suspects finished at most 8 years of schooling, and one-fourth of them are classified as having a "primitive level of culture and intellect" by the experts. (We don't know what that means.) This clashes with the fact that certain people do not know how to leave the country illegally or evade military service in a practical manner. Or they do not know how to choose their words when they talk to the police who are proceeding against them. If we recall that it was determined that alcohol influenced events in 40 percent of the cases, then it is obvious under what conditions these "culprits" have "incited" against or "insulted the community." Those drowning themselves in alcohol in pubs and fast service bars are at the mercy of the system. In the shadow of the debate about state-supported alcoholism, the uneducated drunkards are exposed to police tyranny and provocation.

Occupations of the Suspects

	Cases	Percent
Skilled worker	141	24.7
Semi-skilled	51	8.9
Unskilled	140	24.6
Professional	38	6.7
Employee	38	6.6
Independent	14	2.5
Retired	20	3.5
Student	64	11.2
Dependent or Without Occupation	48	8.4
Other	16	2.8

Even Dr. Kovács mentioned that workers make up more than 50 percent of the suspects, and of course, a large number of retirees are workers, too. In addition, he is talking about "good workers."

There can be no complaints about 60 percent of the "agitators."

Then why do they convict so many workers for agitation and insulting the community?

The reason for the large proportion of laborers in the following table can be explained by a law enforcement practice which seeks to avoid involving the intellectual class when it comes to political cases. Condemnation of the "handful of political dissidents" is a repeated theme in the speeches of officials. However, they do not press political charges against us. Instead, they refer to various other infractions, such as "violating the press law" or "bungling." They want to avoid the publicity caused by political trials, which would damage the image of Hungarian socialism in the West. But they punish spontaneous and unorganized expressions of discontent with trials that exclude publicity, thus keeping the lowest segment of society in check.

Relationship of the Suspects to Work

	Cases	Percent
Likes to Work	122	21.4
Does His Job, Does Not Like It	17	3.0
Average	199	34.7
Sloppy	82	14.4
Lives Like a Derelict	80	14.0
No Data	70	12.3

Workers are not protected by international public opinion. They are more at the mercy of the state, since they do not know their rights or how to defend themselves. But it is not only easier, it is more important to strike at them since they represent the masses, and the masses mean power. The main purpose is that their power should not unite with that of the intellectuals. Let them see that the intellectuals can shoot their mouths off, while they get theirs shut. This kind of animosity is good for the powers-that-be.

Let us at least recognize that Dr. Kovács' article, despite its flaws, is useful, since we rarely see such statistics about so-called anti-state crimes.

43 ANTI-STATE CRIMES
DOCUMENTED IN 1983

Hírmondó 1, 1985

The source is the 1983 Statistical Yearbook. We learn from it that two years ago — the 1984 yearbook is still not on the market — 43 "criminal acts against the state" were committed in Hungary. Action was taken against 23 "perpetrators"; the others could not be tracked down. Eight persons were ultimately convicted, seven of them for agitation, but two were given a suspended sentence. The six condemned and confined to prison received between 2 and 5 years. All of them were men. (The condemned members of the punk ensembles are not included in these statistics; they were legally convicted in 1984). Who were they, and why in reality have six of our compatriots been imprisoned for years? For a facetious remark, for expressing their opinion on a leaflet, or for a student prank with a political overtone? We can only guess.

POLICE CONDUCT ILLEGAL SEARCH OF APARTMENT

Hírmondó 1, 1985

My home is my castle, says the Englishman. I envy him for this. This is what I think as I gaze speechlessly at the detective in civilian clothes, standing, in his socks, on the top of my chest of drawers, searching through my shelves.

How did it happen that the policeman came to stand on my chest of drawers? In a much simpler way than the fiddler got on the roof. It did not require a judiciary ruling, nor a public prosecutor's writ, let alone my consent or invitation. After all I am not the lord of a manor house. It is enough that the district police captain or one of his subordinates decides to do it, and promptly four policemen could intrude into my one-room apartment. After all, though not the lord of a manor, I am a free citizen in a people's democracy.

But why am I playing the innocent, leaving it unsaid that the visit of the authorities had a cogent reason. It was suspected that by abusing the privacy and intimacy of my home, I was storing illegal publications.

It was not a house search, of course. They were merely inspecting my premises. If I were a girl, I would almost think they came to propose marriage to me. Fortunately they did not do this. They did not put a ring on my finger, nor handcuffs on my wrists. Instead of asking for my hand, they want to have my writings, my manuscripts, a few private letters and four or five samizdat publications. They find one copy of each. Well, I try to cheat again and keep quiet about the fact that they have already found four copies of the 10th issue of *Hírmondó*.

The "room inspection" is as much like a house search as one bad egg is like another. A diligent young man searches through my waste basket unfolding every shred of paper. A somewhat older gentleman peruses with obvious interest the women in the photographs of my youth. Meanwhile two of my neighbors are respectfully standing by as witnesses and probably have a poor opinion of me, the silly old man, who dared to believe that something could be hidden from the authorities.

These gentlemen are polite, they do not break or smash anything to pieces, they put back what they have taken out. One of them asks if he can light a cigarette. Please do, here is an ashtray, I answer willingly, whereupon he starts reading my Swiss friend's letter. Later another person informs me in colloquial terms. They are well informed about my diet and what I had defecated afterwards. Maybe he exaggerates somewhat? I do not argue, but rather agree. After all it is not impossible.

But lo and behold, their work is finished, they are packing up. They take away my typewriter, the publications, the manuscripts. It is wrong to write things for one's desk drawer. That drawer is indiscreet. A person who wants discretion, should write in code on tree leaves. I feel robbed, like somebody whose flower beds have been trampled, like someone whose private life has been turned inside out like a pocket full of holes.

This was my small, initimate home. But all this serves me right, great is my sin, mea maxima culpa. I demeaned myself by breaking of the press regulations. But there is no time for sentimentality, my guests are leaving. Like a polite gentleman, I accompany them to the police station, for further discussions . . .

PROTEST AGAINST IRREGULARITIES
AT DEMSZKY TRIAL

Beszélő 9, 1984

Esteemed Minister! Esteemed President!

Complying with the right of citizens to make public interest announcements, we would like to convey the following:

On 24 September 1983, police sprayed tear gas on and struck Gábor Demszky, editor of the AB Independent Publishers, with rubber truncheons. The police harassed him because he protested the confiscation and reading of his private, personal letters. Demszky suffered a brain concussion and external injuries in the process and was treated in a hospital for 4 days.

The police involved were cleared of any responsibility. On the other hand, Demszky was charged with "violence against the authorities." The Budapest Central District Court handed down a suspended sentence of 6 months imprisonment.

More than 100 people tried to get in to see the trial, but the president of the judicial council excluded everyone who did not have an official invitation. The group was thereby limited to people like the two men Lang and Ganz, who said they were machine tool workers, representatives of the Hungarian news service MTI, and other Hungarian authorities. Of those banned from the courtroom, 59 signed and submitted a letter protesting the violation of the principle of open access to a public hearing. They did not get an answer. After a long debate, the authorities let in several members of the foreign press, but they banned Amnesty International, the United Nations Human Rights Commission, and the International League of Lawyers. All of the groups applied for and received visas specifically to attend Demszky's trial.

The court's verdict contradicts the unproductive, meaningless investigation. The charges did not even attempt to substantiate the police version of the story, that Demszky was arrested for speeding, and that he and his belongings were searched on suspicion of a crime. Besides the policemen involved, only one witness corroborated the prosecutor's description of Demszky's actions, but the reasons provided for the verdict raise doubts about the reliability of this witness.

Neither the other witnesses nor the material evidence supported the charge that the policemen suffered any injury.

In Hungary, only *Esti Hírlap* (a mass circulation daily evening tabloid appearing in Budapest) reported on the trial. Using veiled references, the article attempts to turn the reader against the defendant, avoids any mention of the circumstances of the trial or of the defense arguments, and distorts substantiated facts.

Esteemed Minister! Esteemed President!

Unpunished police brutality, a lack of proper evidence, an unsubstantiated verdict and the bias of the press coverage fills us with great concern.

We ask you to secure enough room for the audience, provide enough time for investigation, guarantee impartial judges, and make sure press coverage is unbiased at Gábor Demszky's appeal hearing.

We are looking forward to your kind reply.

> Ottilia Solt
> Budapest 1023
> Komjádi u. 3
> (Signed by 178 citizens)

AUTHORITIES CONFISCATE PRIVATE PAPERS
AND MANUSCRIPTS

Hírmondó 1, 1985

"The confiscation ordered by the authority of the first instance is legal, since the sequestered materials are in part printed matters which have been reproduced without permission, and in part because their possession by private persons endangers the public order." These are the terms by which the Central Police Station of Budapest, acting as an authority of second instance on violations of the law, had justified the rejection of my appeal. I appealed in an attempt to retrieve my notebook, a few private letters and a host of unpublished satirical prose and manuscripts of poetry. All these have been seized by the district police station during proceedings against me for breaking the law concerning printed matters.

Thus I can't keep my notebook with all the telephone numbers and names that I have listed in it during the year, all the appointments and deadlines, for it endangers the public order, although it does not contain any information concerning the acts I am accused of. Public order is also jeopardized by two letters from my friend who lives in Switzerland, which contain dissertations on historical and social topics. Both are entirely private letters. They do not include any call for overthrowing the regime and have nothing whatsoever to do with samizdat publications.

If my calendar and the two letters are so dangerous, how much more perilous are the satirical writings in my possession. Manuscripts have the bad habit of liking to be printed and published. True, they did not appear yet, we did not even find a xerox machine for duplicating them and thus they do not qualify as printed matter, yet the well-founded suspicion exists that they may have served to produce unauthorized printed matter. Thus I am really not surprised that they have been confiscated. I am more amazed that they did not forbid me from ever using a pen and a pencil, since there is a "well-founded suspicion" that I will scribble manuscripts for unauthorized and gravely suspicious printed materials with these tools. I was also surprised and grateful that they refrained from chopping off my right arm, although the suspicion may be "well-founded" that I will handle those tools precisely with that arm, and that they can be seriously suspected of helping to write manuscripts which may be considered the first steps in the production of unauthorized printed material. The justice is as simple as the logic.

If I put myself in the place of the authorities, a prerequisite for objectivity, I am almost overcome by anxiety. Have they not been too lenient with me? Believe me, it is painful to imagine that a brave and a diligent police official may be subject to disciplinary procedures because of me. I am also worried about the public order. It is so fragile, and I bought a new notebook . . .

My only consolation is that though the public order may be fragile, the legal order is all the more firm. Since the articles of the law cannot be perverted. They can be interpreted only one way, that is, always the way the police see it, in every case.

POLICE BEAT MAN WITHOUT WARNING

Hírmondó, 1, 1985

In one of our cities along the Tisza, worker B. B., a construction-industry machine attendant who received his name from a leading figure of the Russian Revolution, was beaten up so badly by police officers that he was unable to work for 10 days afterwards.

"Three or four uniformed police officers appeared on the stairway, and without asking me to prove my identity or admonishing me in any way they began — amidst abusive language — to beat me without further ado. The blows landed on my back, my shoulders, my neck, my head and — after I put my hands on my face by way of protection — my hands, and one of the policemen even jabbed me in the stomach with the end of a nightstick. I fled from the beating toward the apartment house exit, but the police officers followed and continued to hit me all the way from the building entrance roughly 100 meters to the police van. I fell down several times as a result of the beatings, and at such times they made me get up and continued to strike me. When we reached the van, they stopped hitting me and shoved me into the back of the vehicle." Residents of the apartment house had called the police because of a heated argument he was having with his ex-wife. B. B. made a report to the county's authorized attorney general's office, which sent word that the case had been transferred to the county's office of the police commissioner for disciplinary proceedings.

B. B. was subsequently summoned to appear as a witness at the office of the very police commissioner whose officers had earlier beaten him up. The witness interrogation was not much friendlier than the most recent encounter. It proceeded in this vein: "Keep your mouth shut or else I'll flatten you against the wall." In the finding which brought the case to a close it states that 37-year-old Police Staff Sergeant J. N. and 31-year-old Police Sergeant J. L., patrolmen of the city police commissioner's office, committed no crime, because "J. N. and J. L. took measures against B. B. on the stairway and escorted B. B. to the police van by grabbing him from both sides. This is supported by the testimony of witnesses who were questioned."

The police commissioner's office is obviously prejudiced and incompetent in the case, since it claims that the officers did not lay a finger on B. B. and that there are even witnesses to this. On the other hand, B. B.'s mother and aunt, who were questioned as witnesses, testified that they saw the traces of a beating on the body, head, neck and hands of B. B. when he returned home early in the morning. Indeed, B. B.'s ex-wife also stated in her deposition that she saw and heard her ex-husband being pummeled by the policemen on the stairway.

After this, it cannot be known who the still unnamed witnesses are who support the finding of the police commissioner's office through their testimony and who are still shrouded in a mysteriously dim light. After all, did not three other policemen take part in the operation?

TEACHER INDICTED FOR DISCUSSING
TRANSYLVANIA'S HISTORICAL ROLE IN HUNGARY

Beszélő, 1, 1984,
unnumbered supplement

Legal action, an indictment for antistate agitation, will be taken against 48-year old clergyman/teacher József Márton, who taught geography and biology at the Benedictine high school in Győr. The indictment is based on the fact that József Márton used the concept of historical Hungary and during a geography class spoke of Transylvania as a part of historical entity. The police ransacked his residence in the spring of 1984 and confiscated samizdat publications found there.

POLICE ATTACK MUSICIANS AND AUDIENCE
FESTIVAL IN DEBRECEN

Hírmondó, 617, 1984

On Saturday night, 30 June, the international jazz festival came to an end in Debrecen. As they did every evening previously, 100 to 150 Hungarian and foreign youths still lingered there on the grounds in front of the Sports Hall. A few were holding an extemporaneous concert, and the others were listening to them. Police officers appeared out of nowhere and began a shocking maneuver. One of them started to hit the small orchestra's drummer with a billy club, whereupon those present began to sing Lennon's well-known song about preserving the peace. Ultimately, this was too much for the police. The squad cars arrived, and those present were requested to disperse. But the request had hardly been given when the billy clubs started to crack. Those fleeing were struck and cudgeled, German shepherds were used against them, several policemen assailed those already lying on the ground. Those arrested — among them, three seriously wounded youths — were thrown into a squad car and carted away. News of similar police operations arrives continually. How long can this unrestrained brutality against young people be tolerated?

PUNK MUSICIANS ARRESTED AND SENTENCED

Hírmondó, 11, 1984

Dr. Enikő Pusztai of the City Court of Veszprém sentenced the punk group "Szabotázs" to imprisonment for "agitation before a large public audience." The four members of the group—two of them minors — have been in prison since March, where they are now awaiting an appeal hearing. All four are skilled workers.

The group has appeared twice — and only once under this name with these members — at a scandalous punk concert in Győrszentivány on 30 December 1983. However, the scandal and the end of the concert were caused by the group which followed them, "Aurora cirkáló." (They ritually destroyed a few TV sets on stage, among other acts). A police investigation into "Aurora cirkáló" of Győr was begun immediately, and the leader of that group was sentenced to promptly suspended imprisonment. The police officers dealing with "Aurora" heard some mention of "Szabotázs" from a few of their witnesses and relayed the information to Veszprém. In Veszprém no one bothered to start a separate investigation, but charges were brought against the group based on the communications from Győr.

In a series of hearings lasting from June to September, each of the witnesses denied the official record. They claimed that the lyrics attributed to "Szabotázs" on the record books had actually appeared in "Aurora cirkáló" repertroire, and that they had stated the same before the police, and that certain lyrics did not exist at all. One of the police officers appearing before the court admitted that he had "arranged" the fragments repeated by a witness into verse form. The testimony before the court gave proof that due to a blown amplifier, "Szabotázs" lead singer could not be understood at all. Some claimed to have heard English or German lyrics. The court could not produce written lyrics or a recording. The defense attorneys proposed acquittal for their clients, and in a rather unusual move in our country, drew the court's attention to the serious shortcomings of the hearing, even its unlawfulness. However, the facts could not sway the Court of Veszprém. It seems that they will undertake even an imaginary case, if necessary, to divert youth away from the precipitous road to punkdom toward the proper path.

EVERYDAY LIFE

RELIGION

FOUR CATHOLIC CONSCIENTIOUS OBJECTORS IMPRISONED

Beszélő 11, 1984

In 1984, four more Hungarian Catholics requested that their armed service be changed to unarmed service. József Ujvári, 21-year-old auto mechanic of Tököl, was sentenced to a 33-month prison term. József Szever, 27-year-old timber industry engineer of Tata had already served a year before his studies at the university. He has now refused to do his second and shorter service, requesting unarmed service. He was sentenced to 14-months in prison. Gábor Táncos, 20-year-old unlicensed teacher of Székesfehérvár, was sentenced to a 36-month prison term. János Dombi, 23-year-old locomotive engineer of Bánya (Somogy county) also received a 3-year prison term. The first 3 sentences were pronounced in Budapest at the Military Attorney's Office, the fourth in Kaposvár.

These penalties are, without exception, heavier than those imposed in the past years by the authorities. This new strictness is probably connected with the changes in church policies.

APPEAL TO CARDINAL LÉKAI
ABOUT CONSCIENTIOUS OBJECTORS

Hírmondó 1, 1985

Hungary is among the last 6 European countries in which conscientious objectors are imprisoned. They are sentenced by military courts as criminals generally to 30 to 36 months in prison, and after serving their prison term they are banned for 2 to 3 years from public life. Because of their religious and moral convictions, conscientious objectors want nothing more than the possibility of doing unarmed service. This service does not include armed training and bearing arms, the oath of allegience is replaced by a milder oath, and the participants do labor instead.

In the course of the past years, the conflict between pacifist Catholic youth and the opposing church authorities became well-known. Catholic conscientious objectors do not receive any kind of moral and theological justification from the Hungarian church, which claims that in this case they have no right to talk about their religious principles. In a sermon in the Fall of 1981, Cardinal László Lékai condemned all Catholic conscientious objectors. Below is an open letter to him by Károly Kiszely concerning another example of the denial of moral support:

> To László Cardinal Lékai,
> Primate of Hungary
>
> Honorable Cardinal:
> Since your statements indicate that you are unfamiliar with the official tenet regarding conscientious objection against arms and since the conviction of several Catholic believers was based on your statements, I will allow myself to inform you about the official policy of the Church. According to the Church's teaching which is valid everywhere and for everyone without exception:
> 1. No one should take up arms against his moral conviction.
> 2. No one should be forced to take up arms against his moral convictions.
> 3. The Church must always help a just and reasonable

assessment of the conscientious objectors' situation.

I would like to call your attention to the fact that there are legal possibilities in Hungary for military service without arms and oath. The imprisoned Catholic young men did not refuse military service itself (as you have been saying erroneously) but only requested this officially existing form of military service.

The court's reasons for rejecting these requests and for imposing prison sentences were your statements.

I was also detained, under unclear legal conditions, for almost 3 years for "refusing military service," although I never refused.

I ask that you refrain in the future from making your personal thoughts, which directly contradict the Church's policy, appear as official Catholic tenets.

I further ask that in the name of basic humanity and decency you do everything possible to clear the situation of Catholic believers who have been imprisoned and vilified on the basis of your false information.

I am verifying the Church's policy using experts' opinions.

I am sending this as an open letter, since you never seem to be able to reply to letters sent directly.

Budakalász, 20 November 1984

Sincerely yours,
Károly Kiszely
2 Endre Ady St.
Budakalász 2011

INDEPENDENT JEWISH GROUP 'SALOM' DEMANDS TIES WITH ISRAEL, REJECTS ASSIMILATION

Synopsis of open letter dated May '84,
Hírmondó, 6-7, 1984

The fortieth anniversary of the massacre of 600,000 Hungarian Jews should be a time for profound examination of the relationship of the Hungarian nation and Hungarian Jewry. No one can say that this relationship is resolved and cleared up, that there are no longer any signs of the old hatreds, fears, misunderstandings and prejudices. These cannot be eliminated even by the best intended statements of principle.

Assimilation or Integration?

Hungarian Jewry has regarded itself as an organic part of the nation for more than a century. The overwhelming majority were enthusiastic followers of Kossuth in 1848 and they strengthened the camp of the democratic revolution in 1918. For a long time this identification with the aspirations of the nation was accompanied by an affirmation of assimilation, or a demand for a complete merger with Hungarians, an affirmation which wanted to maintain only religious separation. And for those in whose lives religion did not have significance, even this reservation lost its significance.

But whatever the position of Hungarian Jewry in regard to assimilation in the past 100-120 years, historical experience and a new judgment of ourselves justifies a new approach to the problem.

Today, when in democratic states the recognition is gaining ground that it is not necessary to absorb ethnic and cultural minorities but rather to fit them into the society of the majority, that their uniqueness does not weaken but rather enriches society, Hungarian Jewry also must recognize its obligation to itself. When we recognize the right of the individual to assimilation, we should confess in regard to Hungarian Jewry as a whole that it must not assimilate but rather integrate into the society living in this homeland.

Getting to Know the Past

One of the indispensable conditions for a reconciliation between Hungarian Jews and non-Jewish Hungarians is a many-sided portrayal of the Jewish past. It is unfortunate that a comprehensive work about the history of the Jews and especially about the history of Hungarian Jewry has not appeared in Hungary. In general Hungarian historians — a good number of the most famous of whom are Jews! — have avoided this theme, just as the Jewish theme is avoided in domestic politics.

One can observe a curious lack of proportion between Hungarian book publishing in regard to Jewish subjects in the period between the two world wars and in the present — a number of series of Jewish books appeared in the period of official anti-Semitism, they published a Hungarian Jewish lexicon and there were a number of Jewish periodicals. We cannot talk about such things today, and only the pallid and thin *Új Élet*, appearing only every two weeks and frequently delayed, represents the Jewish periodical press. It appears that one cannot even dream of opening a public Jewish library and bookshop.

Our Past Is Ours

It is gratifying that more and more Jewish cultivators of Hungarian culture are awakening to an awareness of their origins and the peculiar traits that they derived from it and are giving expression to this awareness in literary works and memoirs. We must try to encourage this trend, and put an end to the curious practice of not recognizing differences according to origin and treating "religion as a private matter."

Historic Responsibility

After 1945, Hungarian Jews, embittered by the atrocities they had lived through and less trusting of the Hungarian people and of the forces of Hungarian democracy, felt that harsh treatment could not be dispensed with to suppress anti-Semitism and effectively punish those who assisted in the fascist terror, felt that a Soviet presence and pressure were desirable as a guarantee of such a treatment. Thus that part of Hungarian Jewry which did not choose emigration after the catastrophic period of the holocaust fell into a trap of history — by supporting the extreme left and taking a significant part in establishing the Stalinist dictatorship, they only fueled anti-Semitism.

A similar mechanism was at work among a part of Hungarian Jews in 1956 — in their fear of pogroms they were less hesitant to support the Kádár government, during the bloody reprisals following the defeat of the revolution. The excessive brutality against the participants of the revolution could not be justified by their fear of anti-Semitism, since those who were guilty of such prejudice did not constitute a serious political force in 1956.

We must admit that because of all this a certain historical responsibility does burden Hungarian Jewry. But we also must emphasize that a Stalinist dictatorship came into being and operated with similar cruelty in Eastern European countries where the number and role of Jews were a good bit smaller.

In contrast to this we can recognize specific Hungarian features more clearly in the domestic events of 1944. At that time Hungarian Jews were treated more mercilessly than even the Italian Jews in fascist Italy or the Bulgarian or Romanian Jews by the Bulgarian or Romanian henchmen of Hitler. The Hitlerists themselves observed how the Hungarian aid given to carrying out the deportation facilitated things.

The odium of this cannot be passed onto the Germans and the provincial police alone. One cannot dispose of the question by saying that the fascist system was overthrown, that it tormented the Hungarian people too and that the Hungarian people have nothing to do with the sins of the system. It must be recognized and admitted that a certain historical responsibility for the destruction of the Jews does burden the Hungarian nation, and every class and stratum of the nation at that time has a share of this responsibility, if not an equal share. And it must be said that this responsibility is greater than that which the Hungarian Jews must feel for the red fascism of Rákosi or the counterrevolutionary terror following 1956.

This responsibility obliges even contemporary Hungary to develop a special relationship with the Jewish people — just as it obliges the FRG. We will return to this question in the third part of our Open Letter.

Together — For One Another

But we want to emphasize just as vigorously how important it is that the Jews have an awareness of the martyrdom suffered by the Hungarian working people in the course of the development of capitalism, in the First World War, then in the counterrevolutionary Horthy system, during the Second World War and finally at the time of the Stalinist dictatorship. And the Hungarian workers must know that the overwhelming majority of Jews shared in the sufferings with them, a majority made up of little people, even of poor people.

And if we raised our voice earlier that no one should expropriate the intellectual accomplishments of Hungarian Jewry, we must point here to the political accomplishments. The Hungarian people should know the names of those Jews who became victims of the Stalinist terror and the names of those who struggled and still struggle to replace the dictatorship with democracy. There were Jewish victims of the Rajk trial and the other contrived trials. Jewish Miklós Gimes died as a martyr comrade of Imre Nagy, and after 4 November 1956 a fairly

76

large number of Jews were thrown in prison. Jews are not missing from the ranks of the contemporary democratic opposition either. And some of them are molested on the streets by authorities who use "Jew" as an epithet.

But the Jews must be careful not to repeat the error made after 1945. They should develop and preserve their own features, and while their representatives participate in the work and struggles of the Hungarian people at every level, they should also take a stand in their own name in the affairs of the Jews and in the cares of the nation. They should express their solidarity with the just aspirations and national, political and social demands of the Hungarian nation in such a way that in the process their representatives should not set themselves up as the exclusive spokesmen for these demands.

Obstacles to Reverence

On 1 March 1984 *Új Élet* wrote: "Thus far we have preserved the memory of our martyrs in a worthy manner." Still, unfortunately, it is a fact that there is not a worthy monument in a public area anywhere in the country, outside of a Jewish cemetery, which would recall to the new generations growing up the martyrdom of the 600,000 sent to their death. But it is also true that there is no monument anywhere in the country in memory of the sufferings of the hundreds of thousands of non-Jewish Hungarians lost in the hell of the Second World War. The unsolved nature of the problems cutting to the quick of the nation are expressed in this coincidence. The television and documentary film series by Sándor Sára "Chronicle" and "Barrage", touched on this problem correctly, and despite great public interest they were withdrawn and taken off the program.

The government fearfully respects the sensitivity of the Soviet Union. For the same reason there can be no mention of the Swedish diplomat Raoul Wallenberg, the saviour of thousands of Hungarian Jews, who as a "reward" for his self-sacrificing activity in 1944 disappeared into the depths of the Gulag. This is why no one officially remembers Hanna Szenes, who faced the firing squad of the Arrow Cross at the end of 1944 as an English paratrooper who came from Palestine to save Hungarian Jews. And this is why there can be no mention of the fate of those Jewish members of labor battalions who were made Soviet prisoners of war, individually or in entire units, after they had escaped the German death camps.

II. Hungarian Jewry and the Hungarian State

Loyalty to the Nation

Far be it from us to equate the counterrevolutionary system of 1919-1945 with the present system. Naturally we highly value the democratic transformation of society which took place between 1945 and 1948, the elimination of racial and religious discrimination and a part of the economic and social changes after 1948. But also far from us is the view that we owe unconditional loyalty to the government simply because no one persecutes us as Jews today. On this basis Jews would have to be eternal partisans of the government in every country where the government does not conduct an anti-Semitic policy.

Institutional Guarantees

When we recognize that we enjoy equality before the law as Jews, we must point out that the rights of the entire Hungarian nation, of Hungarian citizens as a whole, are deficient. At present it is in this way that we satisfy the obligation of loyalty to the nation.

Phony Game

It is necessary to remind everyone — the propagandists and apologists for the system and those to whom the propaganda is addressed — that the full legal equality of the Jews is not a socialist achievement. It was realized for Hungarian Jews even in the Austro-Hungarian Monarchy. And it is a reality in contemporary western democracies as well. So he who expects, indeed demands, on this basis that Hungarian Jews should support the existing system without reservations is playing a phony game.

Power Interests

Finally, we might point out that if religious freedom of Jews has been realized in our homeland, let us add that in no less but in no greater degree than that of other congregations, this is not yet the same as full freedom of conscience, which is a broader concept. As such, it includes the right of the individual and the community to maintain and cultivate one's traditions and preserve and express oneself. Today, when for various reasons religion no longer plays its earlier role in the life of the average man and when the masses of Jewry are also less and less religious, this means that discovering and realizing secular Jewish inheritance and cultural traditions must be made possible. Thus far, however, neither the state nor the leaders of the Jewish congregation have recognized this important fact in Hungary. In the West it is self-evident.

III. Hungarian Jewry and Israel

Just Self-Esteem

1. The catastrophic — Hitler era and the state of Israel born from the cataclysm mean a crucial change in the life, awareness and emotional world of the scattered Jewish people. What appeared possible before these events is now impossible. One can no longer believe or make anyone believe that self-renunciation and passive surrender are the Jewish fate or a path which can be followed. And the 50,000 Jewish partisans and resistance fighters fighting with weapons against Hitler in various countries, (a significant number of the Hungarian partisans in France were Jews), the Warsaw Ghetto uprising and the Jewish army which stood its ground in the war of independence and defense of Israel have put an end to the slanders spread about cowardly Jews.

After the 6-day-war of 1967 this change reached a new qualitative level world-wide and was recognized.

Every Jew could straighten his back and feel that he was a head taller. The relationship of the Jews to their own immediate and more distant past changed. With all its faults, Israel is blood of our blood, an essential source of our self-esteem, a source for the survival and renewal of our Jewishness.

Defensive Solidarity

Is it not the natural right, indeed moral obligation, of Hungarians living abroad to support Hungarian sovereignty and aid the just struggles of the Hungarian nation? And is it not the right and moral obligation of the Hungarian state and of Hungarians living in the mother country to protect the Hungarian minorities living in other countries, to encourage their national culture! In the same way it is the natural right and moral obligation of scattered Jewry to defend the statehood of Israel. Similarly it is the right and moral obligation of the state of Israel to raise its voice against the grievances of Jews anywhere in the world.

But let us go farther — it is the obligation of every believer in freedom to support the sovereignty of other states against a possible attacker, because freedom is indivisible. It is understandable if the sons of a nation or a people stick together, but solidarity is the right, indeed the obligation, even of those standing outside ethnic bonds. The survival of Israel is the interest of freedom-loving Hungarians just as much as is the preservation, indeed fulfillment, of Hungarian sovereignty the interest of Jews.

Biases

In connection with Jewish solidarity we must turn to a few biases.

Even the Jewish religion prescribes support for fellow believers, especially the poor, but even independent of this religious prescription, it is a natural right, indeed requirement, that a community, nation, ethnic group, congregation or association, should strengthen solidarity among its members.

The second bias is that solidarity, the way "the Jews stick together," is incompatible with pluralism, with the multiplicity and democratic struggle of interests, opinions and tendencies. Let us proclaim unity against the dangers threatening our existence, unity in crisis, but freedom and multiplicity in interpreting the subordinate questions, if this existence is not in danger. And because unity can be realized when it must be.

The third bias is that loyalty to the Hungarian nation clashes with solidarity toward Israel. This is an error. The two are not contradictory in the same way that sympathy with a people defending its freedom and independence fits in very well with patriotism.

The claim of the Jews that they can be loyal to their homeland and to Israel at the same time has long been natural and recognized in the West.

The fourth bias is that solidarity with Israel means the same thing as support for the Israeli government in office. This is a groundless assertion. No one among the Jews living in the diaspora is obliged to agree with another or with the Israeli government in the detailed questions of Israeli politics.

Human Contacts Instead of Cold War Relations

The citizens of Israel of Hungarian origin need the treasures of Hungarian culture and the Jewish citizens of Hungary might be enriched in their Jewishness if they could get to know the creations of modern Jewish culture unfolding in Israel. The Hungarian homeland could only gain if its culture were to spread to the Near East and if its Jewish citizens were to grow stronger, in humanity and in their linkage to the country, by virtue of their enrichment in Jewish culture. Universal Hungarian culture would gain by all this and might be embellished by additional unique colors.

One or two tiny, bashful steps have been taken in the area of cultural contacts, but the foreign policy dependence of this country on the Soviet Union is hindering their unfolding. This also is why Hungarian public opinion, including Hungarian Jewish public opinion, has heard only slanders and one-sided, distorted instead of objective information about Israel in the past decades.

In connection with this a few words should be said about the responsibility of the Jewish reporters and commentators of the Hungarian press, radio and television. Those who give their Jewish names to the cold war campaigns against Israel disgrace themselves. Rather than proving their objectivity, they prove only their spinelessness. And the Jewish TV commentator who reviles Israel should not believe that his listeners do not recognize the Jew in him. Such behavior only arouses disgust in men of good feeling, even if they are not Jews.

Old Anti-Semitism in New Guise

We cannot close our eyes to the fact that in the wake of the initiative of various dictatorships and bloody tyrannical regimes of dubious moral standing which have come to power in the developing countries, and with the zealous support of the Soviet Union, Israel has been forced into positions in international politics of the sort that the reactionary domestic political circles of several countries intended for the Jews in earlier times — they have been proclaimed the scapegoat, the cause of every trouble, the devil's disciple.

It is only natural that in this way "anti-Zionism" can serve as a disguise for anti-Semitism epitomized by Hitler. A good illustration of this is the number of outrages committed by Arab or pro-Arab terrorist organizations in recent years against the temples and institutions of Western European Jewry.

Palestinians and Transylvanian Hungarians

The past, historical responsibility, obliges Hungary to have a special relationship toward Jewry and Israel.

It is an absurd phenomenon that the Hungarian government, which is inclined, in regard to Israel, to recognize at most that every state in the Near East area must guarantee its security — it does so without mentioning the name of Israel — and which in the 36 years of the existence of the Jewish state has never seen a reason to speak up for the millions whose existence is threatened there, should take a stand for the right of Palestinians to an independent state.

The above-cited behavior of the Hungarian government is all the more curious since this same government has been unable, since the elimination of Hungarian autonomy in Transylvania, to publicly demand its restoration. During official solidarity campaigns each year any other people will sooner be mentioned than Hungarians in Slovakia, Transylvania or the Carpatho-Ukraine.

Realpolitik?

It is impossible not to recognize the effect of dependence on the Soviets, and Soviet pressure in the Hungarian government positions on Israel. The question is: "Is this the only form of realpolitik for a

Hungarian government today?"

And is this the only realpolitik for Hungarian Jewish leaders, one realized in hossanahs for the regime and a cowardly abandonment of solidarity? Should it not be demonstrated, and would it not be sympathetic in the eyes of the non-Jewish Hungarian masses, that there is a different Jewish position besides the one of György Aczél and Ernő Lakatos, the leader of the Agit-Prop Department of the Central Committee, of Péter Rényi and Pál Ipper, and of Chief Rabbi László Salgó, who embraced Arafat?

It would be preferable to have a Jewish position opposed to the royal ideology, obtrusive propaganda and foreign policy servilism, a position which might tie together freedom of thought, developing democracy and protection of national and nationality interests.

What would happen if the leaders of Hungarian Jewry, or at least the majority of them, were to raise their voices in public for a settlement of Hungarian-Israeli relations? Would they all be arrested? That would be a worldwide scandal. Or would they only be made to resign? But who would take their place?

Settlement!

We feel that it would serve international detente, the peaceful coexistence of states with differing social systems and beyond this even a peaceful resolution of the Near East problems — and Hungary might be given a certain role in this too — if Hungary would:

• restore diplomatic relations with Israel;

• build up normal cultural and economic contacts with Israel;

• take care of furthering undisturbed human and family contacts among citizens of the two countries, putting an end to travel restrictions;

• open up free tourist traffic.

The fortieth anniversary of the terrible destruction of 600,000 Hungarian Jews is a sufficiently serious occasion for us to think about all these things. And it is sufficient reason for us to give voice to our desires and our anxieties as well. In doing so we desire to serve both social peace and international detente.

OPEN APPEAL BY MEMBERS OF HARASSED RELIGIOUS SECT

Beszélő Special Issue 2, 1984

The writers of this statement are seeking the goodwill of Hungarian public opinion since they have been harassed by certain officials and have only experienced indifference on the part of those authorities responsible for handling such matters.

Our Christian sect, God's Assembly, which is being reorganized, is comprised of a charismatic, fully evangelical congregation. Because of the growth in our numbers and official reaction to this increase, in September 1983, we submitted our organization's bylaws to the president of the State Office of Church Affairs for approval.

When our request remained unanswered, on 7 June 1984, we asked Pastor Tibor Iványi, president of the Evangelical Brotherhood, to provide legal sponsorship for our congregation. We notified the president of the State Office of Church Affairs of this step in writing.

We received no official response to this letter either, but the official harassment we had experienced over the past several years continued. Some members lost their jobs, some had their apartments searched, while others were subjected to minor police harassment on several occasions at our places of worship. In the No. 10 1984 issue of *Magyar Ifjúság* (Hungarian Youth), the weekly of the Communist Youth League (KISZ), Ágnes Seszták attacked us in an extensive, slanderous article.

It was a shocking incident involving the widow Mrs. József Galambos, who has a serious heart condition, that prompted us to write this statement. She is a member of the Reformed Church and has close ties with members of our congregation. On 30 October 1984, at 11 o'clock in the morning, two men, both in their 30's, came to her apartment in Balatonfüred at No. 3 Népköztársaság Street and asked to be let in, saying that they came from Budapest.

The unsuspecting elderly lady let them in, assuming that they were also Christians. After a quick survey of the apartment, the guests started to question Mrs. Galambos about her connections. When they did not receive answers which satisfied them, they screamed at her and demanded to know why Levente Petrőcz, the son of the Reformed Minister and a member of our congregation, comes to visit her from Budapest with his "buddies." When they received another evasive answer, the two, who affected the manner of officials, began to abuse and slander Levente Petrőcz, whom Mrs. Galambos has known for almost 10 years, along with the leaders of our congregation. They called our fellowship a "Western supported mafia" which could expect extra funds for ensnaring Mrs. Galambos. They declared that "We'll make sure they don't make a catch here."

When Mrs. Galambos said that neither she nor the congregation, is afraid of the police since they are not doing anything wrong, they asked her if she had heard that "some people have inexplicably disappeared, and a few dead bodies have been found in various places?"

The old woman was terribly frightened by this threat. She thought that they may try to kill her right there. They made her promise to break off all contacts with Levente Petrőcz and his "buddies."

After the visit, her health was severely shattered.

We are firmly convinced that this and similar cases of crass atrocities can only happen as a result of the conduct of the State Office of Religious Affairs which failed to respond to the submission of our bylaws, prepared and provided to them according to regulations. Because of our unsettled legal status, we are vulnerable to further harassment and other official abuse. Even if these are perpetrated by individuals (without apparent official connections), such actions do not serve to enhance either the international reputation of our country nor the peaceful coexistence of people with differing world views. Moreover, they certainly do not contribute to an improvement of the atmosphere of violence and tension which is so noticeable nowadays.

We ask the support of all well-intentioned public opinion in the effort to normalize our legal situation so that we may live our lives undisturbed within our religious communities.

Budapest, 6 November 1984

In the name of God's Assembly:

Tamás Havas	Sándor Németh	István Tallér
Gábor Nagy	Levente Petrőcz	Uzoni Péter
Pál Nemes	Ervin Pisztér	Tamás Vácz

MINORITIES

GYPSY MINORITY SUFFERS
FROM NUMEROUS DISADVANTAGES

Abridged version of article by Ottilia Solt

Hírmondó, 6-7, 1984

The so-called "Gypsy debate" was concluded last May in the popular economic magazine *Heti Világgazdasag* (12 March - 12 May l983).

The last representative Gypsy study was completed in the first half of 1970 by a team led by István Kemény, and its result can be found in "Report on the Situation of Hungarian Gypsies on Basis of Research Done in 1970", Sociological Institute of the Hungarian Academy of Sciences, 1976. Among István Kemény's colleagues, sociologist and member of the Foundation for the Assistance of the Poor, Ottilia Solt also contributed to the debate in *Heti Világgazdaság*, but her article was not published by the editors. Our paper is thus making up for this omission.

Sociologists and economists have published a number of outstanding analyses about how the modern Hungarian city exploits the village . . .

Most of our Gypsies live in villages and gradually they are becoming the principal source of cheap (rural) labor (that commutes on a daily or weekly basis to the capital).

Whoever writes or reflects about social welfare for Gypsies, and declares that there is enough of this, perhaps too much, should not forget, that the road on which he drives was probably built by Gypsies, or if he lives in a housing project or an exclusive condominium it was probably built by Gypsies. If he takes a walk in the park or enjoys the fresh air at a playground, he is generally enjoying the work of Gypsy hands. Or have the prosperous officials of the Ministry of Labor thought of the fact that when they are enjoying their well-deserved weekend rest, the tennis courts that exist for their recreation were made smooth by Gypsies who travel 200 kilometers for work? I know this because they happen to be my acquaintances. But the builders themselves seldom enjoy the results of their own work.

We can learn from the literature, even if we fail to observe it directly in our environment, that the prospering majority of Hungarian society is not making it on wages and incomes but by taking part in the second economy. Workers living in villages like the Gypsies engage for the most part in household farming through some family membership in a TSZ (producer cooperative). Gypsies are very rarely members of a TSZ. . . Generally, to participate in the second economy, it is necessary to have some kind of material base, for example, a plot of ground, a minimum amount of capital, expertise, connections, and most of the Gypsies do not have these. Those Gypsies who are able to participate in the second economy, are in fact able to prosper.

In connection with my remark about a plot of ground, I want to emphasize that Gypsies received land only as an exception in the 1945 land reform. We know that a significant portion of our poor peasants did not achieve prosperity upon receiving the allotted land, but with their small possessions, they at least had a house and a garden. They had some place to start. Most of the Gypsies never even owned a square foot of land. We must not forget this, not only because of the economic consequences, but because of the symbolism. It was with emancipation like this that the Gypsies started their life in the new society.

Between the two World Wars, balance between the Gypsy and the non-Gypsy societies was upset. We know this to be true of many other balances, and that at the time, a great number of Gypsies and others eked out an existence without jobs. A line of argument which begins with the traditional idleness of the Gypsies is nonsense from the historical-sociological point of view, and it is simply false, besides being ill intentioned.

There are two different points of view and the concomitant unresolved conflicts in the debates that are periodically repeated about the Gypsies. One, which always touches off the debate, more or less blurs the line between the ethnic Gypsies and those speaking the Gypsy language, seeking for the Gypsies nationality rights on a linguistic basis. The other, represented by József Vekerdi, denies the existence of a Gypsy native-language and refering to linguistic diversity, rejects the nationality approach.

"Nation" and "nationality" are political categories, and while they have and may have something to do with language, language is in no way their precondition. I believe there are many Austrians who would protest the view that the Austrian nation does not exist because their language is German. The same goes for Americans, Argentinians, and so forth. Most likely the Welsh would object if their national existence were questioned because only a few now speak their ancient language.

It is a matter of common knowledge that Gypsies are a discernible group of people whose ethnicity, language or anthropology is not the object of much attention. It is obvious, for example, that those who expressed their various opinions on the "Gypsies" in this debate were not constrained to give an explanation. In fact, we are also informed that official, and not least of all, public statistics are being prepared on the Gypsies. One of the debaters has sounded the well-known alarm: the Gypsies are multiplying many times more rapidly than "Hungarians." Other debaters reassure him: they are not so prolific, for among other things the infant morality rate is, reassuringly, higher. No one disputes the fact that the Gypsies have fertility, demographic, employment, and crime rates. Therefore, the majority of the population, including official institutions, differentiate this ethnic group without having any doubts and they do not ask for an opinion about this question. Does this attitude only dispute political existence, or the right to become a nationality? Yes, it can do so, for nationality is a political category. There have already been examples in Hungarian history of the political suppression of ethnic minorities, the word "nationality" is a product of this. There is one political nation, the Hungarian, the others are nationalities. The results are well known.

Acceptance of the nationality rights of Gypsies would obviously not solve the social situation of hundreds of thousands of Gypsies, their disadvantages in the labor market, or emancipate them. A nationality organization can be a completely empty and formal matter. In fact, Hungarian Gypsies, given their present condition, would be able to create only a weak, inefficient organization. But the Gypsies' own community organization is the only institutional possibility for them to control and to defend themselves against a differentiation independent of their will, and to gain human dignity without denying their ethnic existence.

Whether the Gypsies would succeed in realizing their nationality efforts and turn the nationality organization to their own benefit depends, among other things, on how they choose their allies, and how they accept those who offer to become their allies.

Whether or not there is or will be such a struggle, it has the support of all their countrymen who think democratically, although above all it is the Gypsies who immediately have something to win or lose. The democratization of the entire country will be advanced if this society, perhaps for the first time in the nation's history, accepts the equal existence of its largest minority group.

Budapest, 1 May 1983

HUNGARIAN FROM TRANSYLVANIA ASKS ROMANIAN EMIGRES FOR COOPERATION

Hírmondó 6-7, 1984

My Dear Friends,

Please forgive any stylistic or grammatical errors I might make. I left Romania 6 years ago and Romanian is not my native language.

I shall talk about the Hungarian question in Romania. You are acquainted with the situation: differentiation based on ethnicity, a decrease in the number of schools using Hungarian as the instructional language, propaganda campaigns to stir up nationalistic sentiments, and so on. And it would be better not to mention the past: history books with lies — Hungarian official lies before 1918 and Romanian official lies after 1918 intended to justify the injustices committed against the minorities — poisoned the sources of experience to such an extent that I would not believe it would make any sense at all for us to try cleaning the water which we must drink day after day. Therefore, I shall merely rely on a few generalities which you too surely view as evidence. This evidence belongs to the very essence of our civilization derived from antiquity and Christianity.

Thus I take it for granted that you do not deny the right of the individual to political, economic and religious freedom or the right of a group to choose a winning way of life and — above all — together with me, you believe in the overpowering force of love for our neighbor.

I think that every alert and open mind will draw similar conclusions from this simple evidence — and here I could close my letter and could express my conviction that we do understand each other with respect to these basic and elemental questions. However, as I cast a more-or-less pious glance at the state of affairs, some skepticism is justified.

Therefore I should like to spell out — although perhaps much too concisely and briskly — what I would like to propose jointly with you for remedying the complaints of Hungarians in Romania, both in Transylvania and elsewhere:

• cultural autonomy in the sense proposed by the social democrats of the old Austro-Hungarian Monarchy and radicals of the type of Oszkár Jászi and Vasile Goldis; bilingualism according to the Swedish model in Finland;

• territorial autonomy through regional decentralization the way it was planned by Gaston Deferre and his ideological friends in

France, or with improvements proposed by the Catalanian CiU (Convergence and Unity) Party in the wake of the Spanish regional reform;
●that intolerable borders be rationalized as expounded by Titulescu [Romanian secretary of foreign affairs between the two World Wars, a liberal politician — Editor]; emigration liberalized and direct cultural and political interaction between Romanian citizens and foreigners promoted;
●that the existence of national minorities as distinct, separate entities with their own separate, cooperative-political bodies in the framework of a federalism blending the cultural and regional autonomies be assured.

Of course these proposals cannot be implemented as long as the Ceausescu family and the organization serving them remain in power. By the way, they are a power decisively maintained through the chauvinistic frenzy of their own kindling. It is your duty to contemplate Romania's future, to find the road out of the bankruptcy, and to prevent the chaos which will arise at the collapse of the system. And this chaos could lead to another 1907, to pogroms, [in 1907 there had been a peasant uprising claiming 11,000 lives and also pogroms Ed.] and to a dictatorship of gendarmes either with or without Russian help. Your historical duty is to voice a profession of faith, ending the century-long national animosity, which also includes forgiveness and atonement of sins. I am convinced that only repentance can lead to a tolerance which is something more than indifference. Let us forgive each other the past, dear friends, and let us proceed forward.

I know that the sufferings of the Hungarians in Romania represent only a part of all the injustices tormenting the country's population. I know well that the exorcism of nationalistic hatred can be realized only in a democratic, free and peaceful Eastern Europe. But it is our task that we begin at least the effort toward reconciliation and understanding. It is possible that we will not live to see the happy results of this effort. Nevertheless, I feel that we have no time to waste.

My God protect you, my dear friends. Although, of course, I have no formal mandate to say so, nevertheless, you must know that you can count on the solidarity of the Hungarian democratic opposition in the cause of every noble goal and also that we shall not forget about our share in combatting the murderous stupidity called nationalism.

Budapest, 5 May 1984

With brotherly regards,
Gáspár Miklós Tamás

COMMITTEE TO SUPPORT CHAMPION OF MINORITY RIGHTS IN CZECHOSLOVAKIA

Hírmondó 11, 1984

Dr. Miklós Duray has been struggling in defense of the rights of the Hungarian minority in Czechoslovakia for more than a decade. In his latest appeal addressed to President Husak in February of this year, he warned about the risks of the new Education Bill aimed at eliminating Hungarian and other minority languages as a teaching language in the so called national minority schools.

Public opinion in Hungary has been sympathetic and attentive to the struggle in defense of the rights of the Hungarian minority in Czechoslovakia. When Dr. Duray was first arrested on 10 November 1982, many letters of protest were sent to the governments of Bratislava and Prague and many people appealed to the Hungarian government asking it to intercede on Dr. Duray's behalf. As is known, Dr. Duray's trial was then eventually suspended and the defendant was released.

Dr. Duray was again arrested on 10 May 1984. This is when the Duray Committee was set up and its formation was soon followed by an appeal asking Hungarian citizens to do whatever they could to get an innocent victim of persecution out of jail.

Throughout his civil rights campaign, Dr. Duray has always adhered to constitutional rules, and any sentence against him would therefore amount to a grave violation of human and civil rights. Such a sentence would also be an ominous precedent, since in the history of the national minorities living in Czechoslovakia and Hungary, this would be the first political prison sentence in a national minority case since 1948.

Despite protest coming from the most diverse sources — from well known Slovak intellectuals to renowned American writers — Dr. Duray is still under arrest and awaiting trial.

Hungarians also raised their voices. Three Hungarian writers released a statement to condemn Dr. Duray's arrest. Responding to the appeal of the Duray Committee, individual citizens and groups have sent letters to the Embassy of the Czechoslovak Socialist Republic in Budapest or asked the Hungarian leadership to intercede in letters addressed to the government of the Hungarian People's Republic and the Central Committee of the Hungarian Workers' Party.

There would have been in fact several opportunities to intercede.

Hungarian party and government leaders have often met their Czechoslovak counter-parts during the past 6 months. The press has regularly reported on meetings on different levels, including the summit now under way. All these meetings have not affected Dr. Duray's position. A man struggling for the respect of the constitutional right of the Hungarian minority in Czechoslovakia is awaiting trial in prison while Mr. Gustav Husak, invited by Mr. János Kádár, is paying an official visit to Budapest.

The Duray Committee will continue its activities until Dr. Miklós Duray is set free.

27 November 1984

The Duray Committee:

György Bence	Gyula Benda
Mihály Hamburger	Bálint Nagy
Erika Törzsök	János Vargha

CULTURE

HELSINKI KITSCH

Article by Miklós Haraszti

Beszélő 15, 1985

The Cultural Forum ended without the participants agreeing on a closing document. Thus, seemingly nothing happened that did not disappear without a trace once the Forum ended.

In meetings held in private homes strong words were spoken against censorship, even if they could not be spoken in a hotel. Police surveillance of the underground publisher Dr. György Krassó was terminated. Passports were finally given to samizdat intellectuals who previously had been forced to stay home. They allowed some emigrants to come into the country who had previously been forced to stay away. Starting precisely on the first day of the Forum, Western newspapers could be seen at some newsstands in the city center.

The domestic press did not mention any of these steps. Nevertheless, they were an implicit admission that all the restrictions which were now relaxed were unlawful, un-European, and anti-cultural, and that they could easily be terminated.

But who can remind the authorities of this admission, once the holiday is over and only the holy trinity of the central party organization, the cultural police, and the Soviet embassy remains on the scene? And even if it had been possible to agree on a closing document, what would have made the communist countries adhere to its stipulations any more than they have to the Helsinki agreement? Today there is less cultural freedom in every Eastern European country than there was at the time of Helsinki, and if Hungary is an exception, this is not the result of the "Helsinki process."

Therefore, after the Cultural Forum, is everything the same in Europe as it was before? No, the essence of this strange conference remains with us.

Certain things undeniably happened. Totalitarian and democratic countries held a conference about the future of culture, with the intention of reaching a consensus. Also remaining with us is the technique with which the conference was carried out; that is, the use of secret diplomacy, which before only the socialist countries had used for cultural ends. Also remaining with us is a new concept of culture, whose birthplace actually isn't Budapest, but Helsinki.

If the young (György) Lukács was right, culture is nothing more than development of the desire to perfect ourselves. In Budapest they took a big step, purely by the very existence of the Forum, toward a very possible accomplishment: a common official culture for Yalta-Europe. I call this new culture Helsinki Kitsch, and I suggest that, like the desire we feel to perfect ourselves, it lives and has an impact, even if for now no closing document was achieved.

That the Forum could take place at all is due to the fact that not two, but actually three sides were represented. Two Western points of view are concealed behind the superficial solidarity.

Let's start with the East; at least it is united. True, the Romanians and Hungarians try to make it appear that they swing between the two sides, but in fact they took part in the coordinating meetings organized by the Soviet delegation before and during the conference, and pursued the bloc's common goals.

The second group was comprised of not only the neutral, but also some of the NATO countries, which pursued common goals both before and during the conference. These countries wanted to develop contacts across the iron curtain through their official establishments and experts, regulated by the Helsinki process. They tried to assure the Eastern countries that they did not want to weaken the iron curtain by any other means. Obviously, the point that unites them is the fact that they favor official state contacts. As long as cultural contact can be established between countries, they don't care if guarantees of independent cultural activities are violated. They only pursue the original Helsinki philosophy. These countries suggested changes that would make life easier on a humanitarian level, but did not hope to advance the cause of cultural or political pluralism.

On the contrary, they considered such a tendency to be illusory or destabilizing, and therefore dangerous.

The third type of cultural strategy is represented mostly but not exclusively by the NATO countries. They are also not insensitive to humanitarian questions, but a development since Helsinki, the appearance of pluralist opposition, has degraded the politics of detente in their eyes. They hoped that the interest of the East in this Forum would be too strong to permit the socialist countries to remain totally negative about demands for a decrease in the influence of the state. If they wanted to receive festive recognition and admission into European culture through the main gates, the socialist countries would have to show some progress in tolerating non-official culture and undisturbed international cultural contacts.

Naturally their attempts to protect non-official culture is not based on a misunderstanding of the political situation. They obviously don't

believe that, with the exception of Poland, the opposition has succeeded anywhere in weakening the dictatorship of the party during
the past ten years. They want to ensure that authentic underground
pluralism will survive the Communist state, which drives culture in a
different direction, because they still hope that someday a truly
democratic Europe will come into being.

Evidently this would also be the "line" taken by most of the East
European cultural opposition if they could take part in the "Helsinki
process." The extreme position, which would demand that the West
should not discuss cultural questions with the butcher of Afghanistan
and the master of prisons and psychiatric hospitals, would be represented only by a minority. I would agree with Paul Thibaud, who as a
member of the French delegation, represents a hard but constructive
line.

Because of all these factors, the real struggle at the Forum was
not between the East and West, but between the two different Western
points of view. According to the rules of Helsinki Kitsch, it was an
invisible and mute match, which did not end according to the prescribed formula. True, the plan of the hard liners to introduce the
concept of independent culture into the legal framework of the Eastern
countries, precisely the prospect that makes them tremble most, did
not succeed. The Soviet camp counted, and rightly so, on the ability
of those taking the more flexible line to force the hard liners to make
some concessions on principles. But the culture of Europe, which
had been put in the balance by the Helsinki consensus, still did not
tip toward the East.

Nevertheless, the Forum was an excellent example of Orwellian
"newspeak." It was conducted according to the strictly monitored
procedures of socialist television. Not one single Western delegation
was willing to introduce as its own the statement of the democratic
Hungarian opposition, which was excluded from the Forum, or the
letter of Charter 77. But the participants did not have it any better.
They had no right to make their statements public. As a matter of
fact, the official participants had even less chance to make their views
public, than those who were kept out of the Forum.

Before only official Eastern Europe ignored culture that was independent of the state; but on this occasion all of official Europe did
the same thing.

A DECLARATION AND AN APPEAL

by György Gadó

Hírmondó Jan/Feb. 1986

In the most recent issue of the *Hírmondó,* I addressed an open letter to the national headquarters of the Customs and Revenue Police. In the letter I protested against the fact that customs agents took away and confiscated newspapers and books that I had brought with me from the West.

At my home I received a decision, dated 23 December, made by the Budapest Headquarters of the Customs and Revenue Police, which lists (in 14 paragraphs) the 71 books, newspapers, journals and manuscript notes which will be returned to me, then states: "I find no valid reason for the return of the remaining press products." In other words, of the 118 items listed as confiscated from me, 47 have been permanently taken from my possession.

The decision makes no reference to my petition, which I not only made public on the pages of *Hírmondó,* but also mailed to the appropriate office through regular channels. Nor does it explain why it took more than two months, instead of the prescribed 30 days, to close my case. Together with the decision, they brought back the material in question, wrapped in a strange satchel. However, they failed to make sure that it was handed over to its rightful owner, and did not allow the recipient to make sure that all the indicated items were included. (The bundle was received by a sub-tenant temporarily in my apartment.)

In closing, the decision uses as a precedent a certain paragraph of a decree issued jointly by the Minister of Finances and the Minister of Foreign Trade.

I declare that I consider both the cited decree and the substantive and formal circumstances of the procedure to be illegal and deleterious. I continue to protest in the sharpest terms against this application of censorship, this arbitrary limitation of the freedom of information and opinion, and this infringement upon my rights through the confiscation and detention of my private notes.

I conclude that when the authorities confiscate such a literary work of world rank as the novel "Life and Fate" by the non-emigrant, Soviet writer Vasilii Grossman, they bring shame on the cultural policies of the government. When they confiscate Orwell's satire, "Animal Farm," they reveal that the statement made by the insiders of cultural policy-making, according to which Orwell's works "could be published in our country," to be a lie. When they confiscate volumes of István Bibó, they prove that occasional praising references to Bibó in official publications serve only to side-step the issues. When they confiscate a book by Péter Gosztonyi, a historian who lives in Switzerland, they demonstrate that even if the author is permitted to travel to Hungary, he must be muzzled before the public. When they confiscate issues of the Tel Aviv publication, *Új Kelet,* which can in no way be referred to as a counterrevolutionary publication, they make plain the well-known fact, that in the course of the "dialogue" with Hungarians living abroad, the communists can do the talking, while the Hungarians living abroad can only listen — at least in front of the Hungarian public.

I hereby publicly announce that I will take steps to replace the books that have been confiscated from me, and I have already obtained one of them (Zoltán Zsille's "The Autobiography of a Faith"). I propose a movement of civil disobedience in opposition to the illegal decrees representing censorship, and I CALL UPON everybody to do the following:

1. Immediately and decisively protest, orally and in writing, against any incidents involving the confiscation of books and newspapers.

2. If the situation were to arise, insist upon the receipt of a precise inventory involving confiscated material.

3. Anyone from whom any kind of press products have been confiscated since 1 January 1983 (whether while traveling or at home, by customs agents or policemen) notify me of his name, address, and the particulars of the case, so that we can initiate joint action in the defense of our civil rights before the Supreme Prosecutor, and, if such action proves to be in vain, at the international organizations protecting human rights. I am asking the same of all people from whom books or newspapers will be confiscated in the future.

4. Hungarian citizens traveling to the West, and foreign citizens visiting from there, should bring in as many journals and newspapers as well as political and fictional writings as possible. They should be inventive and make it difficult for the illegal censorship to operate by hoodwinking the dogcatchers of free thought. By the very volume of imported press products they should make it impossible for the bloodhounds to perform their repulsive duties.

31 December 1985

György Gadó
H-1117 Budapest
2 Magyari Imre Street

POET FORCED TO RESIGN FROM PRESIDIUM OF WRITERS UNION

Article in *Hírmondó 11, 1984*

The poem "Eternal Summer; I Am a Little Older Than 9" originally appeared in the October 1984 issue of *Új Forrás*, a small circulation provincial literary journal published in the city of Komárom in Northwestern Hungary. The relatively obscure source became notorious because of the poem, and the poem, which may have otherwise gone unnoticed, came to the attention of a wide audience. At a regularly held policy meeting for the "leaders of the press," the party and security authorities brought the poem to the attention of editors, who in turn relayed the information to their colleagues. In this manner, in a relatively short time, a large portion of the country's intellectuals came to know that at least one official Hungarian publication ran a poem remembering Imre Nagy on the 28th anniversary of the revolution of 1956. The journal quickly went off the market, and *Hírmondó* republished the poem to provide an opportunity for a larger audience to read it.

The poem soon became a cause celebre, when the cultural authorities demanded that the poet who wrote it be dropped from the presidium of the Writers Union. The president and vice president of the Writers Union threatened to resign and the subject of the short poem in the little-known publication had developed into a full-scale scandal.

The impasse was resolved by an agreement according to which the poet resigned from the presidium but remained in the Union and was not punished in any other way, at the time of *Hírmondó*'s publication.

the grave

        Is Nowhere   the assassIN

the grave

the body

                        neither HERE

        Is Nowhere

the body   nor THERE

the bone

        Is Nowhere   the assassIN

the bone

(P.S.)

        one day he must be buried agaIN

        and we must not forget him agaIN

        we must call out the name of the assassIN

ECONOMY AND THE ENVIRONMENT

DETERIORATION OF THE STANDARD
OF LIVING CONTINUES

Hírmondó 1, 1985

The standard of living in Hungary has deteriorated for years. From official statistics, it is evident that real wages, which serve as the accepted measure of the standard of living, have declined by 2.9 percent between 1980 and 1983. (Statistical Yearbook, 1983.) As of now, the compensation for the January increases in the prices of basic foodstuffs, sources of energy and transportation have come in the form of promises. In our article, we contemplate as laymen would, and only on the basis of published data, statements and the trends that have been discernible for years, what we can expect in the near future and how the poorest groups of society will be affected by this unpopular measure.

It was officially announced last year that the general price level will rise by 7 percent in 1985. Among the January price increases even the smallest one (the price of books) was 10 percent, that of dairy products 35-40 percent, sugar 16 percent, electricity almost 20 percent, fuels 25-33 percent and local transportation 55-60 percent.

Yes, we know that the general price level is not made up of the price of these few articles and services, and the promise of the government might even be true regarding the 7 percent. But the smaller the income is in a family, the larger the portion of it that must be devoted to basic necessities. For the majority of people, it is doubtful that they can respond to the price increases by moderating their rate of saving and with a modest slowing of the consumption of non-basic products, as was optimistically assumed by the deputy president of the Bureau of Fishing in an interview with *Heti Világgazdaság* (HVG).

When considering the price increases of the most fundamental articles necessary for survival, one cannot neglect those social groups which can least easily provide, with overtime work or the creation of new sources of income, as is done by the majority of our society, for necessities such as food, heating and housing. In years past, given the artificially low wages, pensions and social welfare payments, it was only the price supports that have made it possible to satisfy their minimal needs. Low wages and price supports have produced a self-complementing system. This economic relationship, which makes it possible to live at the minimum level has now been endangered for large economic groups, like old and poor people, unskilled laborers with large families, all of whom, because of their cultural dependence and isolation cannot assert their interests and cannot affect the spiral of prices and wages. For the possible consequences, it is valuable to refer to some results of the research about the poor conducted in the early seventies. These sociological studies have shown that poor families spend 60-70 percent of their income on foodstuffs, while in the average Hungarian family this percentage is only 30 percent. In spite of this, or maybe because of it, the poor are disproportionately more undernourished. They cannot afford three meals a day, on weekdays they don't eat lunch. They eat meat only on Sundays, if at all. Their children don't consume the minimum necessary number of calories. These families usually heat only one room of their apartment, and still their proportion of expenses for heating is high and their money goes in greater proportion for the maintenance of a minimal, supportable temperature than is the case with people having average incomes[1]. One doesn't need a sociologist's knowledge of facts or empathy to imagine to what degree these already miserable circumstances will deteriorate as a result of the present drastic measures. It could be argued that the above conclusions are already out of date and that their logic is unfounded. We get a picture very similar to that of 10 years ago if we look at the latest (1983) household-statistics publication of the Central Statistical Office. For example, in households receiving 1,800 forints monthly in pension and support payments per person, comprising largely elderly poor people, less than half as much meat was consumed, a third as much fruit bought, and even before the price increases, 30 percent less sugar was purchased than in those with a retirement income of 5,000 forints or more. Even today, people receiving low retirement income spend 59 percent of this income on food and services (Housing). The detailed tables have made it possible for us to see, assuming unchanged consumption patterns, what additional burdens the present price changes will impose on these families. The price increase in bread, baked goods, sugar, sweets, heating and energy (other items having experienced a price rise are not listed separately in the tables) will require an additional 100 forints expenditure per month, per person. The minor pension supplement of 80 forints will therefore be swallowed up by the current price increase and there will be no reserves left for further increases in prices. It is no exaggeration to say that the pension supplements are more to pull the wool over the eyes of the public than to be an effective means of social policy.

In even more distress are those hundreds of thousands, mostly families with many children, who don't receive any kind of compensation. Because they do not have a steady job, they do not have a right to the 80 forints of family assistance (GYES), the new child support supplement. They pay directly and without any compensation for the costs of the improvement of the country's balance of payments, and it is rather unlikely that they had a role in causing the disequilibrium.

Of course, when confronted by inflation, everyone thinks of his own pocketbook, looks for new sources of income, calculates, grumbles and inquires about the prospects of a pay raise. Those with double incomes or working in the "domestic farm" sector or in other branches of the second economy can adjust by raising the price of their own products or by increased exploitation of others or themselves. In the area of compensating mechanisms and in asserting one's interests, a few characteristically Hungarian ways have been developed. He who cannot get involved in these processes because of a lack of professional training, capital, or family background, say, one who belongs to a group of social dropouts, will not be party to the conniving glances and will not be helped by the Hungarian magic phrase, "Dig old boy, you'll find your share."

These people probably cannot applaud the fact that the present price increases will improve the budget by 60 billion forints, but even the person who is not threatened by hunger may not have cause to rejoice. In vain has the government lowered consumer price supports by billions for the last 6 years. In the same period, state support payments to companies and public outlays have risen by a larger measure. It appears therefore that whatever is saved by the belt-tightening policy that affects the people on the one hand, is lost by the companies and agencies on the other. Billions are put into the bottomless pockets of the large companies, and are swallowed up by state and enforcement agencies. It must also be noted that because only the main indicators of the budget are published, the public is not informed with due thoroughness and accuracy about the state economy's expenses and income. It must argue on the basis of obvious facts. For example, take the fact that the quality of education and of health services is catastrophic and that money is surely not spent on these but on something else. We can also detect a new element in the preparatory propaganda campaign. Instead of the usual explanations, the balance of payments has a deficit, etc., but alongside the "accurate forecast" of the yearly price increase, the government has now promised that the deterioration of real wages, which has been occurring for many years, will be stopped this year and that the price increases will be compensated for by a 7-7.5 percent rise in earnings.[2] Other things have happened behind the scenes as well. The mass media have produced the appearance of an extraordinary wheather crisis in January. Every day, energy experts and high-ranking government figures have given statements to journalists that the lack of oil, natural gas and coal reserves have necessitated austerity measures. All this was accompanied by the effective crescendo of shortening television programming which required the sacrifice of nighttime movies. Thus public opinion in the country has completely succumbed to an austerity psychosis. In any event, it seems that the shortening of TV programming has produced small savings but has instead created the political advantage that the attention of the population was shifted from prices to the energy shortage.

Whatever the energy and fuel situation, the population has noticed the price increases. Capital gossip has it that it caused several disturbances in factories, and protest leaflets were distributed in public places. True or not, these rumors express people's desires. Maybe even the patient Hungarian populace will not accept its continuing exploitation without a word of protest.

FOOTNOTES

[1] Knowing these relationships, it cannot be a coincidence that the poorest social strata have regarded the price increase of energy carriers in particular as producing the most severe impact, according to an opinion poll in January.

[2] Of relevance is a poll of public mood made at the end of January, according to which the public was shocked by the size of the price increases and 95 percent of the inhabitants of the capital do not believe that the rise in wages will cover the rise in the cost of living.

ECONOMIC REFORM SERVES INTERESTS
OF MANAGERS AND PARTY, NOT OF WORKERS

by Gábor Demszky

Hírmondó, 1, 1985

Superficially it looks like the state and economic leadership of Hungary are making an opening toward more democratic forms and procedures. The election reform instituted last year and the reform introduced this year for enterprises made political gestures in two directions. However, the "great reform steps" mean quite different things to the two groups addressed: those who are interested in reform, or simply want just to believe in it — here I include western public opinion, where a prejudiced image of Hungary as a model country of reform has already spread — and the workers, who are the ones who suffer from the repressive decrees and the reduced real income that accompany reform measures. The two groups are separated from each other so far in practice, that people belong only to one or the other.

If, because of managerial neglect, lack of expertise, wasteful management and bad decisions, market-place recession — and especially the bankruptcies of recent years — work places must be reorganized, the workers can easily end up in the street. And what do they receive in exchange for increasing uncertainty? Certainly not a strong union that would defend their interests even against enterprise management. There has been no talk of trade-union reform, or strengthening the safeguarding of interests along with increased risk and exposure, by giving more independence to the organizations that safeguard interests. One could only hear of public meetings at small companies and delegates to the councils of middle-sized enterprises.

But only one group of members of an enterprise council represents the workers. The others are either named by management or are ex-officio members of the council. The enterprise's party secretary has the right to participate in the council, as do the secretaries of KISZ (Communist Youth Organization) and the trade union. But the opinions of these functionaries must be sought out also in the process of naming workers' representatives. The criterion for appointment is reliability, and the governing principle that previous social activities of those names must also be taken into account serves to insure that political demands are met. (In regard to this, see the joint governing principle of the Council of Ministers and the Central Council of the Hungarian Trade Unions', *Szakszervezeti értesítő,* December 1984). It is not probable that real representatives of the workers will make it thourgh this sieve. We should not rely on this, if for no other reason than that for such a thing to occur many other things would have to change. The workers would have to see a chance that they really could have an influence on decisions that affect them. The other side's advantage in information and strength is alarming, and in the new council, workers will be in the minority from the offset as compared to the managers, who are more competent on technical matters. There can only be genuine debate if outside, independent experts are listened to.

But even the possibility of being watched has aroused anxiety among enterprise managers, and since the party decisions directing the new forms appeared, they have been working untiringly for an organization to safeguard their own interests, a so-called union of socialist manufacturers. Professor Tamás Sárközi spoke about this at the journalists' conference held in April of last year at Tihany: "The interests of enterprise managers will be represented within the Hungarian Chamber of Commerce. There was a great debate about this: The Chamber did not want to undertake it, because it did not come within its legal authority, and they were correct about that. The Chamber is an organization that represents the interests of the enterprises only, not those of the enterprise managers. But the enterprise managers do need to have their interests represented, therefore the Chamber must do it." And it did — even before the formation of the enterprise councils. True, it was not within the bosom of the Chamber, but within the Patriotic People's Front, as a forum for information and uniting opinions of the enterprise managers — (HVG — *Heti Világgazdaság,* 12 Jan. 85). Articulation of interests is thus proceeding well on the one side, but we have unfortunately heard nothing about the formation of a national "information and uniting forum" for workers' representatives.

It is not worthwhile dreaming ideals into the changes. It appears from the minutes of the preliminary negotiations and from the legal provisions already worked out that the ideology of the reform was conceived in the spirit of marketing and decentralization. Nothing is said about self government and worker control. Those who formulated it had in mind not economic units built from the bottom up with contractual agreements but strong and independent direction by managers. Self government plays no role in the documents, it is at most mentioned derogatorily, citing the Yugoslavian example, where "the team-work organizations . . . without party and state went bankrupt" (Tihany Journalists Conference).

As the new enterprise management forms were being worked out, it was not clear for a long time to whom some of the rights of ownership and the responsibilities should be transferred. The goal was just that enterprises be shifted from management to the worker collective, as long as this works. If it does not, the state liquidates the enterprise." (Quotation from materials of the above-mentioned conference.) At first they thought that delegates to the council of a middle-sized enterprise would come from three places: state organizations (ministries and banks), mass organizations, and the enterprise's management team. During the debate, this solution was rejected, and the opposition camp argued that the enterprise council could not make decisions binding on independent organizations in any case. Local leaders, management cadres, and representatives of the apparatus were left, and to these workers' representatives were added.

On the basis of the changes that are now becoming clear, we can only repeat and strengthen the thought stated in the introduction. The ambiguity that is noticeable in social life and — in the case of our example — in the field of economics is frightening. The new forms the have been introduced will clearly increase vitally important uncertainty, but they will not guarantee articulation of the interests of endangered groups. The illusion is democratization, the reality is increased influence for managers and the local party organization. The managers are safeguarding their own interests even before the starting point, whereas the workers' representatives are recommended by the party.

MINIMUM INCOME IN HUNGARY

Beszélő 15, 1985

In 1984 a committee worked, in deepest secrecy, on the question of what is the essential minimum income in Hungary. The committee's work was coordinated by the National Statistical Office. Also taking part in the project were the MSZMP Central Committee's economic policy division, the National Planning Office, the Finance Ministry, the State Wage and Labor Office, the Ministry of Health, the MSZMP Central Committee's Sociological Institute, the Economic Institute of the Hungarian Academy of Sciences, the National Council of Trade Unions, the Trade Unions' Theoretical Research Institute, the State Youth Committee, the National Council of the Patriotic People's Front, and the Communist Youth Organization's Central Committee. In addition to working out the essential minimum income, the coordinating committee also worked out the "social minimum" that is enough for a modest but socially acceptable existence.

We wonder, why is the minimum that is necessary to our citizens kept secret from them? Maybe because it would be painful to compare it to the average wage level of workers, and even more painful to compare it to pensions, family supplements, and child allowances. Would it perhaps become clear that the legal wages paid for work done during the legal number of hours do not cover the essential minimum needs of a family? But maybe the government wouldn't like to have the governed start brooding about what is covered under that minimum, which is still not minimal enough to be assured to everyone. We also wonder why the government bothered to figure out a "social minimum," which means a significantly higher standard of living, when it can't even guarantee the bare minimum to each person. Could it be for the sake of international statistics?

Let us examine the amounts they established.

Monthly Income (in Forints) Necessary for One Person

	Year	Active	Inactive	Total
		Members of Households		
social minimum	1982	2470	2210	2430
	1983	2640	2330	2590
	1984	2850	2550	2800
	1985	3040	2760	2990
essential minimum	1982	2010	1840	1990
	1983	2160	1950	2130
	1984	2330	2130	2300
	1985	2490	2320	2460

In 1985, the minimum corresponded to the following percentage of the average income

	Active	Inactive	Total
social minimum	66	60	—
essential minimum	54	50	—

If we compare this to the National Statistical Office's latest (1982) figures on income, we see that 19% of the population has income below the "social minimum" and 7.3% below the essential minimum. A fourth of all families with three children did not achieve the social minimum, and more than half of families with four children failed to achieve it. Fifteen percent of retired people who live alone have income that does not reach the essential minimum, and the average pension of widows covers only 90% of the essential minimum. Similarly, average wages, together with the family supplement and child allowance, only cover 90% of the essential needs of a couple with one or two children. We should also note that in effect the minimum is decreasing, since yearly increases in it do not keep up with the rate of inflation.

According to the National Statistical Office figures, 780,000 people have income below the essential minimum. We are not in a position to debate about the accuracy of these data, but in any case we would like to call attention to the fact that even according to these official statistics, hundreds of thousands of people live far below the essential minimum. After all, the essential minimum is 9840 forints for a family of four and 12,300 for a family of five, and the income of village gypsies does not come anywhere near this level. But other groups also fall far below it: village families that have one income and don't own a dwelling, the families of disabled unskilled workers, and families that have to depend on the income of unskilled women workers.

It is certain, however, that the situation is even worse than is indicated by the official statistics, because the official minimum is based on the needs of households that are already established in an independent dwelling. Aside from a lucky minority, most Hungarian families take 8 to 10 years to get their own place to live, and during that time they restrict their spending as much as possible. This means that at any given time a fourth or fifth of the working-age population is suffering through the years devoted to trying to establish a home. If we subtract the cost of saving or building, and the cost of furnishings, we find that a further 7.3% of the population has less than the essential minimum to spend.

The official minimum figures also seem very doubtful when we take into consideration what kind of "consumer's basket" the committee assembled. According to their calculations, those who live on the essential minimum only have to spend a third of their income on food, and they still have something left over from their housing expenses for the "other necessities" category, clothes and transportation. The only trouble is that the "consumer basket" is quite unrealistic. For an adult worker it allows 3050 calories per day, but a man who does hard physical work definitely has to eat more.

GROWING PROTEST AGAINST GABCIKOVO (BŐS) — NAGYMAROS DAM SYSTEM

Article by Gyula Dénes

Hírmondó 67, 1984

Numerous articles have already been published in the Hungarian press about the harmful consequences of the planned system. The investment would cost Hungary 43 billion forints, and yet this sum still does not include the sewer construction or wastewater purification expenses of the surrounding settlements or other, also unavoidable environmental protection investments. These will increase it to about 80 billion.

The large amount of contamination which will be deposited and accumulate in the water storage facility will probably contaminate 10 cubic kilometers of drinking water reserves of good quality below the island of Szigetköz. The theoretical value of this water is 50 billion forints. Extensive forests, our best lumber-producing forests in the flood protection area, and agricultural regions, i.e. about 70 square kilometers of agricultural land and about 50 square kilometers of forests, will die due to the lowering of the water table level, since there will hardly be any water in the present bed of the Danube or in its dead branches, dried up by the by-pass channel. The all-time water level of the Danube regulates the ground water level even at long distances away from the river as a result of its thick gravel bed.

The level of the water stored in the Nagymaros storage facility is 25 meters higher than the corresponding level in Budapest and in an emergency this may have catastrophic results even in Budapest. The vicinity of Nagymaros is an earthquake-endangered area. The stone bed has cracks in it. Thus in order to avoid a flood which might occur in case of an earthquake, the reinforcement work for the storage facility would mean additional billions. Also, at high water levels, the water will flow upstream for about 30 kilometers in the tributaries of the affected section of the Danube, and this will carry waste water back into urban areas such as Győr. For this reason certain settlements should be completely equipped with sewers. Today this is an unresolved problem, because there are no financial resources to provide for its solution.

I could keep on listing the obvious and possible damages, I could analyze the psychological effect the construction has on Hungarians of the Csallóköz island. A portion, in fact a major portion, of the productive lands of Nagybodák, Vajka and Doborgaz has been confiscated and the villages have in essence been sentenced to death since they are being squeezed between the channel and the old riverbed of the Danube. We could count on extended Slovak settlements, which now means working hands for the construction projects, together with lifetime housing and department stores stuffed with the "most excellent" merchandise, but along with it, we can also count on eventual Slovak monolingualism in this region.

The size of the investment is a reminder of the practices of the 1950s. But while Hungarian society simply lost money on uneconomical investments of that and of later eras because most of them never paid for themselves, and indeed their operation has been costing heavy millions ever since, this present investment endangers the fundamental interests of society and of the country.

All the debates, discussions and lectures held in the spring of this year proved that the only unconditional supporters of the investment are the National Water Management Office and those engineers and officials who are directly interested in the project. It has also come to light during the debates that they cannot give answers to all the varied environmental protection and profitability questions which have come up. Their answers are cynical and supercilious. Instead of reason, their words ring with the pompousness of those in power. Not one water management expert was able to provide a reassuring reply to the question, could the success of this investment be guaranteed after the unsuccessful investments on the Tisza river.

The investment will consume huge amounts of money. The return, if there is any, will be minimal. The damage caused by the construction is incalculably extensive and it increases the threat of a catastrophe in the region. Why is the system being built then? Partly because construction has already begun. Even though this answer may seem absurd, that is the answer we received in many debates about this problem. "Because the contract has been signed, because an international contract is involved here, because if the contract was cancelled, the relationship between the two countries would deteriorate, because much money has already been spent on it." In our economic situation, not one single answer was heard which could have tangibly justified an undertaking promising such "dubious" results. This may be why a black-out has been ordered on all news about the project, and this is why further public debates have been prohibited.

1985 ELECTIONS

REPORT FROM BUDAPEST
ELECTION DISTRICT NO 13

Hírmondó May/June 1985

The first nominating meeting was held on 18 April 1985 in IPARTERV (Architectural Designing Enterprise for Industry and Agriculture), 10 Ferenc Deák Street, 5th District; the second, on 2 April 1985 in MOGURT (Foreign Trade Enterprise for Motor Vehicles), 38 Váci Street, 5th District.

László Rajk's candidacy unquestionably has been and will remain the most troublesome self-declared candidacy.

Already his name grates on the official ear. And to boot, he is a member of the democratic dissident movement. Furthermore, he has been proposed as a candidate in an election district where there are universities, and the students are eligible to vote. It was to be feared that irresponsible young people may make a deputy out of him if nothing were done!

The first nominating meeting was called to order to 5:30 pm on 18 April. Its site was IPARTERV, Rajk's place of employment. This meeting had been scheduled for the very beginning of the nominating campaign. That is perhaps the main reason why it was a surprisingly staid and peaceful meeting. Instructions may not yet have been received from above about what to do if someone wanted to intensify the already growing danger of democracy.

IPARTERV, the site of the meeting, should have given Rajk the advantage of running on home turf. But the boss, the director of IPARTERV, sat at the chairman's table! So Rajk's colleagues, with the exception of the most determined ones, felt that it was more prudent to go home. Their departure freed seats in the small hall. Unlike at subsequent meetings, even the supporters of the independent candidates found seats here.

The ample room and comfort also revealed that neither side had mobilized seriously for this occasion. Or if they had, then their mobilization was low-key, without serious political content. Each of the official PPF candidates, both directors general close to retirement age, had evidently brought along a group of their subordinates. This may not be entirely regular, but it is understandable. Nobody likes to lose, and nobody likes to leave things to blind chance. This applies to dissidents as well. We sent word to a friend or two. University students also hung up a few posters. Someone quickly removed these. The dissidents themselves did not conduct any serious pre-election propaganda. There were differences of opinion as to how sensible it was to run in such an election. And to tell the truth, we ourselves did not take the whole thing all that seriously.

This is how it came about that there was a relatively large number of people in the hall who had not been bought in advance, either on the left or the right. But not even they were the "people." It is indisputable that the present electoral system is not as demeaning and as lacking in good taste as the old one. In spite of its weaker ability to repel, however, most people still preferred to stay away from the electors. On this occasion the public was the traditional one of state and social events, retired party workers, social activists, elderly ladies, and persons who prefer, for unfathomable reasons, to spend their time at official ceremonies. Mobilized Stalinists kept this public from subsequent meetings, but they were still present here.

Naturally, this subculture within the movement also frowns upon the likes of Rajk. It was the more surprising, therefore, that Rajk won a few votes even from this segment of the audience. In all he received the votes of 40 percent of those present, more than the required one-third. With a modest margin he was able to make it to the next round. All together, there had not been that many colleagues of the nominees, tipped-off sympathizers, dissidents, and students in the hall. I may be exaggerating if I attribute a third of the votes to them. The rest of the votes came from the other camp. It is unnecessary to lose ourselves in detailed mathematical calculations. Anyone there saw what happened.

This phenomenon is not easy to explain. In the interview with Rajk, the reader will find the main planks of his platform: referendum, unrestricted publicity, and end to government by decree, autonomous public initiatives, and similar things.

One would have thought that all this would have evoked disgust, protest and scorn from the party and PPF activists who were present. But hardly anything like that was encountered. If the mood in the hall had any common denominator at all, it resembled curiosity rather than enmity. It seems that when party control of feelings and passions is not firm enough, such vacillating and scattered reactions, or indeed votes for dissidents, may emerge even from the movement's activists. I am unable to prove it, but the entire atmosphere of the meeting suggests that Rajk would have obtained many more votes, but for the presidium at the chairman's table and the other observers in the hall.

The majority, nonetheless, held on to socialist reality. After a brief uncertainty, the distancing from László Rajk began. We lack the space to cover the debate in detail. The dissidents, sympathizers and students said more or less the same things that Rajk had said. The objections to Rajk may be classified into two groups.

Here the pro-Kádár, state-conservative objections were still in a majority. Rajk was viewing the socialist world through dark glasses, magnifying the mistakes and belittling the results. He failed to take the existing conditions into consideration, and to appreciate the achievements. He had not demonstrated his goodwill and done enough voluntary public work. His criticisms was abstract, and he was not advocating cooperation to solve the existing problems. Therefore he could not possibly be a good deputy.

A smaller proportion of the objections followed the Stalinist line. "László Rajk was paying lip service to the conditions set by the PPF, but actually rejected them." "Let him empty his pockets and reveal his misdeeds!" "There seem to be a few State Security cases in his background!" "How does such a guy dare to aspire to a seat in the National Assembly?"

These Stalinists hopelessly confused the election with a police interrogation. They failed to understand that in the given case a public "confession" extracted from Rajk, i.e., disclosure of the details of the situation and of how the secret police operate, might perhaps not be detrimental to him. Had Rajk yielded to this goading, the ideological row would indisputably have been greater, while he would have held on to his votes as well. But Rajk did not succumb.

He came not to list the dissidents' grievances, but to offer a platform from which, he believed, society would benefit.

In this election the PPF proposed for nomination Dr. Pál Gagyor, the director general of the Industrial Information Science Enterprise, and Nándor Paisch, the director general of the Volán Trust. Both men are in their fifties and are members of the district's party committee. They did not offer individual platforms, although Dr. Gagyor did indicate that he would concern himself mainly with research and development, and with improving the situation of the technical intellectuals. And Nándor Paisch talked about the problems of passenger and freight transportation, and the resulting environmental damage. It was felt that he had been selected as the sacrificial lamb for the dual nomination, and therefore mostly he won the dissident votes.

The official candidates, however, gave us the least trouble. Under the present system, the candidates are not immediate rivals and may move on together into the next round. The directors general patiently answered the pro-dissident questions. Sometimes, evidently in their confusion, they said also a few peculiar things. They pledged to enhance the National Assembly's authority, to free the Constitution of the flood of lower-order decrees, to broaden publicity, and to protect the environment even through referendums if necessary. All this as a trend, of course, not hastily but deliberately, in accordance with the possibilities and with due consideration for the overall situation.

There was also a fourth candidate, Dr. László Sárdy, an attorney and an activist within the district PPF. He was a bit late. By the time he was given the floor, the audience was already tired because of the fight over Rajk. Therefore he deemed it best not to trouble the audience any more. What little he did say revealed a progressive young man who is an excellent speaker and irreverent toward the play staged by those who wield power. Among other things, he told the official candidates to come down from the speaker's table and to take their places in the rows. With this he won the wholehearted empathy of the dissident camp and its votes.

Tibor Fekete, the district's party secretary, was not in a position to emulate Dr. Sárdy's example and spare the audience. When everybody thought that they could now vote and then go home, Fekete began another lengthy speech. Many regarded this speech as an irregular denunciation of László Rajk. Our assessment is milder. Perhaps the party secretary had received instructions only at the end not to let Rajk run without any comment. Or perhaps he remembered János Kádár's advice at the party congress: engage the loud-mouthed enemy when and where he appears, instead of complaining afterwards in the corridor. But the party secretary was perceptibly unable to decide with what intensity to attack Rajk. The publicity that Rajk was urging was not the publicity that *Népszabadság* or *Magyar Nemzet* was constantly widening. Therefore this question deserved some thought, the party secretary said, while persistently avoiding the word "samizdat."

There probably were voters in the hall who did think things over and decided it would be better not to vote for Rajk after all.

The 223 persons present voted as follows:

Dr. Pál Gagyor	130 votes or 58.3 %,
Nándor Paisch	142 votes or 63.7 %,
Dr. László Sárdy	94 votes or 42.2 %,
László Rajk	90 votes or 40.4 %.

Note: Percentages add up to more than 100 because voters could vote for more than one candidate.

Had this been the only nominating meeting, all four candidates would have gotten on the ballot. But there was still the second round. At the next nominating meeting, Rajk and Sárdy dropped out under circumstances that were suspicious, to say the least. Public opinion is now concerned only with this second meeting. Yet the first one, too, is not without its political lessons. There the rectification that later permeated everything, the ordered turnout, and the artificially generated anti-intellectualism were still absent. It was not obvious at first glance who would be voting for whom. And actually the appearance of a well-known dissident in this first, solidly inimical, environment did not cause such a terrible shock. Not even the fact that Rajk was on the ballot, as things momentarily stood, created a state of general excitement. To use the party secretary's own words, this too deserves some thought.

The indications are that those who wield power did indeed stop to think about this case. And they came to the conclusion that Rajk had to be stopped at all cost!

The way to achieve this was simple. Rajk's supporters had to be kept out, and the hesitating voters had to be deterred. The technology of keeping supporters out was perfected in the course of the nominating campaign.

On 22 April, however, at the second nominating meeting where Rajk was a candidate, the technology of keeping supporters out was still in a state of flux. The cadres who had been ordered to attend occupied the MOGURT headquarters (where the Petőfi Cricle had met at one time) hours before the start of the meeting. But the doors were left unlocked. Informed of the meeting one way or another, a large proportion of Rajk's supporters, mostly university students, managed nevertheless to get into the hall. The election organizers were pained to see that their prudent foresight had been in vain. The situation was still not developing in their favor.

It would be a pity to record the speeches and the contributions to the debate. The turnout of cadres had not come there, hours before the start of the meeting, to seek intellectual recreation. And the students who were arriving late were likewise quick to grasp what was coming. Rather than an intellectual contest, this was to be more like psychological warfare and heckling.

It was obvious from the very beginning that there was nothing Rajk and his supporters could say that the opposite camp would not consider scandalous. The state-conservative tone in the statements against Rajk was suppressed, and the Stalinist demand to expose him intensified. "What happened to your passport?" someone asked Rajk suddenly. The issue of the Gabcikovo-Nagymaros dams turned into an argument almost independent of the nominating meeting.

A young man began his rather confusing contribution to the debate by addressing the voters as "My fellow Hungarians!" A blond girl kept climbing up the dizzyingly high window grate. Others, sitting on the floor, were amusing themselves by playing some game of chance. Once again, they did not let Dr. Sárdy speak. On the whole, however, they heard out the speakers. The chairman recognized speakers more or less proportionately.

It is regrettable that in the end the chair's dignity and fairness had to be questioned nonetheless. When it came to voting, it was announced that 1,388 persons were present. Some people began to grumble at this point. How did the chair know this exactly, since no headcount had been taken? The university students had been crashing through the door in droves, and it was impossible to count there. Later the ladies who acted as tellers were pressed together in a group and could barely move. However, the raised hands were somewhat more visible. According to the chair, the results of the tallies were as follows:

Final Results of Nomination Meetings

Candidate	Total Votes	Second Meeting (%)	Total at Both (%)
Dr. Pál Gagyor	873	62.9	62.3
Nándor Paisch	809	58.3	59.0
Dr. László Sárdy	383	27.6	29.6
László Rajk	378	27.2	29.1

Note: Percentages add to more than a 100 because voters could vote for more than one candidate.

These results meant that the official candidates were on the ballot, but the independent candidates dropped out. This development not only violated the interests of the independent candidates' supporters, but it also seemed somehow to conflict with the proportions of raised hands. Shouting erupted immediately. Some people demanded a check, while others questioned the headcount of the voters present. Yet others requested those who had voted for the independents to stay in the hall, for a voluntary recount.

The chairman and his staff refused any check or recount, hastily packed their belongings and left. A young man, who seemed to be a student, shouted: "After them!" A proportion of the voters who had voted for Dr. Sárdy and Rajk remained in the hall. The volunteer tellers counted them only approximately, because their efforts no longer mattered. Between 350 and 370 persons remained. Meanwhile, people were coming and going constantly in and out the door, and the lights were being switched off and on. However, there were also more far-sighted individuals around. They posted tellers at the exits to count the number of persons departing. According to the two separate groups of tellers respectively, 1,064 and 1,115 persons left the building up to the time that the gate was locked.

If we take their headcount and assume that the official tallies of the votes were correct, then Dr. Sárdy (with 35.7 or 37.1%) and Rajk (with 35 or 36.4%) just managed to win the one-third necessary for nomination. The fact that the tellers arrived at different headcounts in the confusing situation, with people coming and going, and the lights being switched off and on, speaks mainly for their honesty.

It is a matter of faith, of course, who regards which data as authentic. Those who wield power will keep insisting until the end of time that their figures are the right ones. And the independent candidates' supporters will keep insisting that there was fraud. This writer likewise leans toward the latter assumption. The headcount was not announced at the start of the meeting, evidently because it was not known. During the proceedings, however, there was ample time to estimate approximately how many Rajk supporters had forced their way into the hall. Anyone there could see that helpful hands were constantly passing notes to the chairman's table. The size of the turnout ordered to attend was known in advance. Furthermore, one could more or less tell that a well-fed man of 50, wearing a jacket and tie, would probably vote against Rajk; and that someone in his twenties, decked out with chains, beads and feathers, had come most probably to beef up Rajk's supporters. The two rival camps that evening were clearly distinguishable in space, age and external appearance. It was enough to estimate the size of those who appeared to be the minority, and you had the tally of the votes for Rajk. From there it was only one more step to find the correct denominator. And let us not forget that the persons sitting at the chairman's table were not there for fun. They had strict party orders.

Incidentally, there were also less prejudiced observers at that meeting. For example, a research group of lawyers also visited the meetings to monitor the fairness of the elections. The following is an excerpt from their report:

"Meanwhile, there is a complete babble of voices. Those who sat in the middle leave. The ones who voted for Rajk stay and occupy the seats, leaving about 50 seats empty. A count shows that there are between 350 and 360 of them. Thus there could have been 420 seated voters at most. All but about 50 or 60 of those standing voted for Rajk. That gives a maximum of 900 people. Where are the remaining 488 people? The fraud is quite obvious to everyone. We believe that there were only 900 people present. Yet the chair established a headcount of 1,388."

In other words, these monitors introduce yet another set of figures and suspect even greater fraud than the people who were close to the dissidents.

And yet the organizers of this meeting must be judged less severely than the organizers of subsequent ones. Here at least the organizers left the doors unlocked and laid themselves open to accusations of having juggled the results. If nothing else, they definitely enhanced thereby the entertainment value of the meeting. The noisy brawls between elderly Stalinists and arrogant students, the persistent efforts of those in power to hold on to their positions, and the honorary presidium escaping with the doctored final results in their pockets, all this enjoyably differs from the Byzantine rigidity of the traditional, Soviet-style ordination ceremonies. A bit of election fraud is something we can still live with. The tendency to cheat in elections is a part of European civilization.

Later on they simply locked out the opposition camp. The democratic forum reverted into an exclusive party event. The excluded now quarreled not with the supporters of the official candidates, but with the police and secret police. The usual scenario followed, identity checks, surveillance in the streets, and arrests. With this the journey into democracy was more or less over, and we were back home again.

This is a logical consequence of the entire evolution. It follows from the nature of the power structure in general, and from the present Electoral Law in particular. The provisions of the present Electoral Law essentially elevate the nominating meetings to a decision-making situation. The earliest possible occupation of the hall in which the meeting is to be held will thereby become the most important objective in the election. This election logic leads to infinity in a pejorative sense. The new type of hero in our time, the expert hall-occupier, now shows up only 3 hours before the meeting is scheduled to begin. But what will happen when the political stake increases? Then he will have to appear 30, 300 or 3,000,000 hours sooner. He can feel truly safe only when he has succeeded in planting in the hall also the guards, the australopithecine hominids, lemurs, pulmonate fish, and diatomaceous algae. Otherwise the enemy might sneak in and vote him down.

Obviously, only determined, militant minorities are willing to assume such burdens. Where someone like Rajk or even a more moderate dissident also decides to run, there the mobs of the ideological fringes will converge by definition. Members of the majority, the nonpartisan population who have weak political motivation and are only slightly interested, will flee in alarm even from the vicinity. Indeed, not even the more moderate party members are inclined to wait breathless hours, just to be able to make denunciations for a few minutes. What will then become of the majority principle, and of popular representation? This question would be justified even if the dissidents, and not the Stalinists, happened to have the keys to the hall and the capability to order larger turnouts. For the general lesson of the nominating campaign is that primarily the Stalinist factions are being activated under regulations that complicate the election process. At most, they are not the ones who run the official candidates. But the Stalinists are showing the greatest affinity for the decisive instrument of their approval, the early occupation of the hall by force.

Of course, these nominations could also be conducted differently. For example, by making the publication of individual platforms an early task, instead of the occupation of the hall. Or by requiring candidates to qualify for nomination by gathering a specified number of signatures from residents in the election district. Naturally, there would be meetings, debates and quarrels even so, but without deciding the election there on the spot. Without the necessity of such a decision, the debates could perhaps become more meaningful.

But there are also other ways in which the question of nomination could be decided. For example, the nominees also could be chosen at a completely closed party meeting. And then, unlike in László Rajk's case, it would not even be necessary to doctor the results.

INTERVIEW WITH INDEPENDENT CANDIDATE LÁSZLÓ RAJK ABOUT THE 1985 ELECTIONS

Hírmondó May/June 1985

Hírmondó: Democratic dissent interprets parliamentary government quite differently from what goes on in the Hungarian National Assembly. And yet you have now joined the election melee. What was your reason for doing so, and was it worthwhile?

László Rajk: Everything considered, I think it was the right thing for us to do. There were both short and long-term reasons for doing so. Viewed in the very short term, we could not afford to miss an opportunity to expound openly, and under some legal protection, the ideas that we have wanted to expound for years. Since, even though there is samizdat and there are communication media, the confusion in the minds of people is enormous about what dissent is, what dissidents are doing, and what their more or less completed platform is. This was a very good opportunity to clarify things, to dispel at least some misinformation.

The Electoral Law, no matter how confusing, has opened a small gap. When such a gap opens, some actions ought to be initiated in the course of which people will learn how they can act, how much freedom they have, and where the pitfalls are. Such events leave a lasting impression in one's memory, and these are the impressions from which traditions evolve. And once traditions have evolved, it is difficult to undo them. Had we contended, without first testing it in practice, that the Electoral Law is confusing and merely a manipulation of power, then our contention would have rested on a very shaky foundation. Now that we, and not only we, have tested the Electoral Law, its true face is revealed. For so far it seems that not a single candidate can get on the ballot who has a definitely progressive platform. Such a candidate will not get into the National Assembly not because they fear that he might get the necessary votes, win a seat, and then become a nuisance. No, what they fear is the one month preceding the balloting, when the nominated candidate has the right to make campaign speeches. What they cannot afford to allow for the time being, or perhaps ever, is such frank and uncensored campaign speeches.

By trying out this test-your-strength machine, we have demonstrated at a cost only to us that the Electoral Law is not meant to be taken seriously. Had we not tried to win nomination, it would have been more difficult to call attention to these shortcomings.

Hírmondó: But it was very specific fraud, and not the law, that kept you off the ballot.

László Rajk: More than likely the law may also have prevented my nomination. For no one knows how the committee which ratifies the results of the nomination meetings functions. I suspect that we probably will never know the answer to this question, since I am afraid that not a single progressive candidate will ever reach the stage of his being considered by this committee.

Hírmondó: The possibility of running as a candidate existed also in the preceding national election, yet you did not run. What has changed during the past five years?

László Rajk: We did not have a platform. Since then we have more or less formulated a platform. It is not comprehensive or detailed, but now it can truly be called a dissident platform if you like. Moreover, this platform is even in the minds of people who cannot be called dissidents. Perhaps some of the planks are lacking, or are formulated differently, in their minds. On the whole, however, something has been formulated in this country.

In other words, to run as a candidate five years ago would have been merely a joke. But now all kinds of seriously considered platform speeches have been made, by dissidents and others.

Hírmondó: Have you imposed any restrictions on yourself when you write your platform speeches? After all, you had to face an audience entirely different from the one we have become accustomed to.

László Rajk: Actually I did not abandon any subject. I did not say everything I should have said, solely because of the time restrictions. And I regret very much that the contributors to the debate did not say these things instead of me. There was only one issue on which I exercised self-censorship: the events of 1956. I spoke figuratively only here. But I did so intentionally and accept the responsibility for having done so.

Hírmondó: What was your platform? What did you speak about?

László Rajk: I spoke about our serious economic situation, from which only the economic reform's continuation can provide a way out. I demanded institutional safeguards that would make turning the reform back impossible.

I spoke of the environmental damage, and the Gabcikovo-Nagymaros dams on the Danube in particular. I proposed that the plans for such large-scale investment projects, and here I mentioned also the Paks Nuclear Power Plant and the National Theater building, be submitted to a referendum for approval.

On the issue of poverty, I spoke of the problems of retired persons and large families. I proposed the establishment of a Ministry of Welfare as a single central agency to coordinate such matters. And I also proposed that the poverty level be determined officially, and assistance up to the poverty level be guaranteed for everyone in need as a civic right.

I demanded that the regulations on forced labor be rescinded immediately. (The impressions I gained while watching the faces of my audience were very strange. People are not aware that forced labor has been reintroduced in Hungary. As an indirect effect of our candidacies, people may now start asking questions about forced labor and will want to know what is actually happening.)

About Hungarian minorities living beyond our borders, I said that the government should finally confront this serious problem. The volunteer work that now exists in Hungary ought to be utilized. The government is neither supporting such work now nor taking advantage of it. I spoke of the need for practical, financial and cultural initiatives, instead of bombastic speeches.

In general, I called attention to the enormous growth of volunteer work in Hungary in recent years. It was through such initiatives that the issue of the Nagymaros dam and the issue of poverty were raised. For every plank of the platform, I emphasized the need to rely on public activists and public initiative, and the fact that it should be the duty of National Assembly deputies specifically to support such initiatives.

Instead of the Presidential Council's law decrees and the decrees issued by the Council of Ministers, I demanded the restoration of the real legislative role of the National Assembly.

Among the problems of (Budapest's) districts, I called attention to the housing situation and to transportation. I proposed changes in credit policy for financing housing construction. Present credit policy cannot be maintained under a housing-construction plan that shifts the main burden of construction and maintenance costs onto the population. And it is simply ridiculous that increases in the prices of building materials have not been included in the computation of the standard of living.

As far as transportation is concerned, I objected to the plan that continues to concentrate in the downtown area not only all Budapest traffic, but essentially the traffic of the entire country. I said that although there is also need for the Lágymányos Bridge, the Budafok Bridge further downstream ought to be built first to relieve the traffic of the district and of the capital. (It is interesting that an article in last week's *Magyarország* claims that both bridges will be built simultaneously. Nobody in his right mind believes this.)

Hírmondó: What was your impression: Was your audience's response to these local and professional issues the same as to the planks of the dissident platform or were you able to win the audience's support with these issues?

László Rajk: At the second meeting, where I dwelt on these issues in greater detail, the contributors to the debate already were very clearly divided. There were young people who spoke up in my support. They responded less to these issues and discussed mainly the Nagymaros dam. The other side's response was that I was throwing around spectacular numbers. But my impression from the general mood of this meeting was that what I had said had been clearly understood.

Everyone realized the catastrophic situation that has arisen even in the 5th District (center of town) where 43 percent of the population is living in apartments that lack a kitchen or bathroom. Then what can the situation be like in the 9th District? The answer to this was merely that I tend to view things pessimistically. At the first meeting, where the audience had not been so well conditioned, these technical issues probably won me a vote or two.

Hírmondó: What was the make-up of your audience?

László Rajk: Relatively few people attended the first meeting. If I am not mistaken the total attendance was 223. This meeting was held at IPARTERV (Architectural Designing Enterprise for Industry and Agriculture), my place of work, but the fewest people came from there. About sixty or seventy university students attended. As it turned out, many people were sent to the meeting from the workplaces of the two official candidates, both directors general. These people remained fairly segregated in the hall, and I believe that they actually came from their own enterprises. The second largest group was comprised of, let us say, elderly party workers. Very few people, perhaps ten in all, came to the meeting, for one reason or another, entirely spontaneously.

Attendance at the second meeting was about 1000. This meeting was organized so that every enterprise in the district was assigned a certain quota of employees to send. For example, IPARTERV, my enterprise, sent ten people. Thus the audience at this meeting was far more mixed, and it was organized far less by the two directors general themselves. Organization this time was a party and council effort. Fairly few people were requested from each enterprise, but the ones sent obviously were among the most reliable. By law, also the BRFK (Budapest Police Headquarters) and BM (Ministry of the Interior) were able to attend, since they happen to be in the district. About 300 university students and 70 or 80 other sympathizers also attended.

I was standing at the entrance from 4:45 to 5:30 pm (that was when the second meeting began) and saw that elderly people, who had come out of curiosity or because of the notice posted at the entrance, stood around for a while in the lobby, but later almost all of them left. The organizers and policemen told them that they could not enter because there were no empty seats left, and therefore they decided to go home. You could say that there were hardly any, or only a very few, district residents there. The ones that were there had been organized by somebody. I can safely say that there was not a single district resident there who came spontaneously, because he was interested.

Hírmondó: Was there any spontaneous electioneering on your behalf by nondissidents?

László Rajk: At the first meeting, one of my colleagues and an economist spoke very strongly in my support. They cannot be termed dissidents. At the second meeting, five or six of the university students spoke in my support, without any prearrangement. Also a woman, a schoolteacher by profession, spoke very forcefully. But there were so many different things to watch, and I cannot possibly remember every speaker. A very interesting thing happened, still at the first meeting. An older man, perhaps I can best characterize him as a trained Communist, perceptibly disagreed with the things I was saying. However, purely as a matter of principle or moral conviction, he said that the nominating meeting's purpose was not to elect but to place as many names on the ballot as possible, so that the voters would be able to choose from among several nominees. Therefore, in spite of the fact that he had criticized me, he demonstratively declared that he would vote for me.

And then there was a lady who seemed to lean more toward the official candidates. But when the question of transportation or of the bridges came up, she realized that it was indeed an important issue. And she sort of defended me when others attacked me for speaking about a general problem that was not the district's concern.

Hírmondó: At the first meeting it was definitely perceptible that you were able to win over quite a few people. In the beginning they were petrified and obviously expected a row. But then they relaxed somehow, and a good many of them even dared to vote for you, even though the district party secretary tried to dissuade them from doing so. Which, incidentally, was entirely irregular.

László Rajk: But I do not think that this first meeting was typical. It did not resemble any of the subsequent meetings. In the course of our discussions, several theories have been advanced as to why this first meeting was one where the formalities were observed on the whole. According to one theory, the Ministry of the Interior obviously knew about the meeting because one or two notices were posted at the university. (These were constantly removed, but the students kept replacing them.) And yet the ministry did not seem to have made any preparations for this meeting. I do not believe that this was because it looked with favor on my candidacy or wanted to observe the laws. I am more inclined to believe that the ministry intentionally held back this information to lend greater weight to its data when it did release them. Another theory holds that the top echelon of the district leadership evidently went to the other meeting, at which Foreign Minister Várkonyi was being nominated. If for no other reason, as a matter of courtesy. And the second echelon assigned to my meeting did not dare assume the responsibility for improvising violations of legality on the spot. This might have been the reason. But it never happened again. Here we may exclude also the possibility that the formalities were observed because of me.

It should be noted that there was also a fourth candidate, Dr. László Sárdy. This is interesting because, by his own admission, he and his friends had decided to test the Electoral Law. Exactly the same way we did, but obviously for different reasons. Incidentally, this candidate is a party member and a member of the PPF. In other words, his career is a fairly official one. And in addition to the fact that he received the same votes that I did, his behavior increasingly assumed dissident overtones. Even we were surprised by some of the things to which he called attention. Among other things, he began his speech by saying that by law all the candidates should be starting with equal chances, yet the two official candidates were already sitting at the chairman's table.

Not only did this candidate receive the votes of our supporters, but he also became a target of the organized audience's dislike. His example is further proof that the people sent to attend the second meeting were instructed to prevent any kind of independent manifestation, whether dissident or not.

Hírmondó: How would you characterize the tone of the meetings?

László Rajk: I think that we all have forgotten the tone of a democratic meeting. Or we have not forgotten it, but do not even know what it is like. Besides being able to present a platform, you also have to endure the actions of your opponents. For in a normal election, one that is democratic or nearly democratic, the opponents do say all sorts of things about one another, and often there is also mudslinging. But this is a part of electioneering. The descriptions circulating in town place too much emphasis on the heckling, on not letting me continue, on the personal remarks, etc. I think this is natural. In Hungary, of course, we are not accustomed to this.

Hírmondó: What angered us the most was that actually you were the only one to present some kind of platform. They did not even let the fourth candidate say much. The official candidates did not present any kind of platform. Essentially the powers that be are ordaining them to sit in the National Assembly. It seems that a person can still flounder into the National Assembly without any platform even now, in spite of the new Electoral Law.

László Rajk: I would turn your statement around: With a platform, one cannot win a seat in the National Assembly!

Hírmondó: Let us look a bit into the future. Will this event have some sort of continuation? What will happen in the next elections?

László Rajk: The next election will be five years from now, and that is a long time. The present Electoral Law will certainly be changed. Changing it is unlikely to be the new National Assembly's first order of business. That would be too conspicuous. Over five years, however, the law will be amended piece-meal, with law decrees of the Presidential Council or by other means. In any event, the present law has to be changed because it simply does not work, either to the liking of those who are in power, or democratically. But we have discussed the establishment of traditions. I think that many people, the university students, for example, have become aware that such a nominating system enables them to choose the nominee. And they are the most active group. All they need is to learn how to run candidates properly.

One thing more about the present Electoral Law. A fundamental contradiction has been obvious in this election. A person either observes the law or disregards it the way his opponent does. Whether you agree or not with this practice is a moral question. The law specifies that a candidate may not present his platform in advance. Only the nominee may do so. This is a sharp contradiction in the present Electoral Law. It is absurd for a person to declare his candidacy, without being allowed to present his platform! Our names alone were perhaps enough for Gáspár Tamás and me. The university students knew approximately what would or could happen. But there were people who were less well known, though they have the qualifications for becoming deputies to the National Assembly. Now, if they do not present their platforms in advance, they are jumping into darkness. This provision of the Electoral Law must either be changed or disregarded, because besides being illogical, it also gives the official candidates an advantage since the organizations are electioneering on their behalf.

Hírmondó: Let us examine some of the critical comments that can be expected. One such comment will probably say that the dissidents, by declaring themselves as candidates, have scorched the field and destroyed the nomination prospects of more moderate reformers.

László Rajk: Events have shown that this was not so. Of course, this critical comment can be interpreted to mean that, say, Ráday or other candidates have not been nominated because we poured oil on the flames. In my opinion, however, in Budapest, no spontaneous candidate can win nomination who does not belong to the district lobby. Because, let us put it this way, the guidelines have been issued centrally, but we must not be so paranoid as to believe that everything has been choreographed centrally. In such cases as the present one, the district does indeed have great power and wide decision-making authority. For example, the order that Foreign Minister Várkonyi must win a National Assembly seat at all costs is obviously issued centrally. But I doubt that there is any central interference in who is to represent the entire district's interests in the National Assembly. For Várkonyi obviously will not be doing that. This other deputy must belong to the group of 10 to 20 people who exercise power in the district. And the district party committee has very extensive supervisory power over all the enterprises and institutions in the district. Therefore I believe that an independent candidate is able to win nomination only when it is evident that he can be brought into this district group. It is logical that I will not place an enemy in a position of power where I have to obtain money or lobby for something.

Hírmondó: Specifically in your case, nevertheless, it was not merely a district action.

László Rajk: Of course not. But I am saying all this merely because I am convinced that even a more loyal reform candidate could not have won nomination. And if he were nominated, then his nomination would have been decided centrally. I too could have been nominated only on the basis of a central decision! This is obvious. And not because the university students wanted me on the list. Simply stated, democracy is not working.

Hírmondó: Is this not in conflict with your contention that the university students could decide who is to be the nominee?

László Rajk: My answer to this question is what I have already said about myself: One can obtain the number of votes necessary for nomination. But the National Election Presidium may still refuse to ratify the nomination, for some perfunctory objection.

Hírmondó: Let us assume that you win a seat in the National Assembly. The general opinion is that you would be isolated and forced up against the wall anyhow. Or, at best, you would be the court jester.

László Rajk: I have ruled out this possibility from the very beginning. It has been demonstrated repeatedly that the time of truly sophisticated, refined dictatorship has not yet arrived in Hungary. The refined tactic of giving someone a seat in the National Assembly to represent the liberal group, and then of isolating him exists only in the minds or hopes of intellectuals. The regime has not yet reached this point, so this possibility has never worried me.

Hírmondó: At the meetings you were constantly attacked for saying that you agreed with the PPF platform. How can you reconcile professing allegiance to the PPF with being a dissident?

László Rajk: I naively believed that a PPF platform existed. I searched for it for days, until I found that there was only the election announcement that appeared on the front page of every newspaper. It consists of a few general sentences and contains nothing unacceptable. However, it depends on how you look at the matter. If we consider the text of the oath of allegiance, its implied meaning, then of course that is unacceptable. But taking only its literal meaning, I will sign it anytime. And, I suspect, any one of us would accept it.

Hírmondó: Has this candidacy been merely an episode in the work of dissent or does it represent something new?

László Rajk: The important thing, in my opinion, is not the future impact on dissent, but that thousands of people have begun to engage in politics for a few weeks. At this stage their stand may not even be important. The simple fact that a large group of people have finally begun to move is essential. And they have not been stirred up simply by the party or the PPF. We too had something to do with this.

Hírmondó: In the final analysis you are regarded as one of the dissidents in the narrower sense. Yet you have supported objectives and ideas that are not explicitly dissenting. What did you really consider yourself to be? Were you the dissidents' candidate, or did you attempt to advocate progress in a more general sense?

László Rajk: I would not in any sense draw such a sharp distinction between dissident and nondissident. These problems are in themselves real and must be considered. Who gives voice to them is of no importance, in my opinion. It may not be an accident that dissidents are beginning to discuss them publicly. But others may raise these problems since, as I mentioned, almost every one of the issues was first raised by public initiative.

Hírmondó: Thank you for the interview.

INTERVIEW WITH INDEPENDENT CANDIDATE
GÁSPÁR MIKLÓS TAMÁS
ABOUT THE 1985 ELECTIONS

Hírmondó May/June 85

Gáspár Miklós Tamás ran as a candidate in election district 14, which is in the 5th District of Budapest. The PPF candidates were Péter Várkonyi, the minister of foreign affairs, and Mrs. József Szabó, director general of HUNGAROTEX (Foreign Trade Enterprise for Textile Goods). Péter Balázs, a department chief of the Hungarian National Bank, was also nominated. The first nominating meeting was held in the Supreme Court building; the second one, in the head-quarters of MOM (Hungarian Optical Works).

Hírmondó: Why did you run? What did you expect of the new Electoral Law? And what was your platform?

Gáspár Miklós Tamás: It was not my idea to try for a nomination. As you well know, it was not "the" dissident movement who thought of this, as many people believed. In fact, certain dissidents were definitely opposed to the idea, some, because they did not want us "to make fools of ourselves," others, because they feared that in the end we would only be generating propaganda for the regime. My friends convinced me to run, even though I knew that the cool feelings toward my humble person which have accumulated within the party leadership promised nothing good. My friends who raised the idea that all kinds of independent candidates should run at the nominating meetings, including the representatives of democratic dissent, felt that the causes and ideas I advocate should finally be presented to a different public. This was an argument to which I could not say no.

My opinion of the Electoral Law is the same as that of any sane citizen throughout the length and breadth of this country. As a gesture, it is significant, but as effective legislation, I consider it to be a deception. I am not alone in this opinion. This is what Péter Schmidt, a law professor, said on *Petőfi Rádió's* "Owl" program. Regardless of how liberal the Electoral Law may be, the professor knows very well that in practice only the PPF's two official nominees can come into consideration, and they offer no alternative. Therefore the law's "pluralistic" guise is a farce. On this same program, Csaba Gombár, the political scientist of the party liberals, openly suggested that even this was too much for significant forces within the party apparatus, and if the leadership intended to continue its (alleged) policy of a democratic opening, then the party apparatus, in his words, would have to be curbed. To this I wish to add that the party apparatus feels reassured by the 13th Party Congress and by the emergence of Károly Grósz. Imre Pozagay, the secretary general of the PPF, also admitted indirectly in one of his public talk shows that what is going on is not exactly an overture to parliamentary democracy.

As to why I "ran," my objective was a political lesson for myself, my friends, and the general public. I subordinated my so-called platform to this objective. Besides environmental and local issues, I focused my attention on controlled democracy. I expressed my amazement that the National Assembly, in two or three sessions a year, each lasting one or two days, is able to responsibly analyze and review the flood of decrees that Hungary's deservedly world-famous bureaucracy produces, while democratic parliaments are in session 150 to 200 days a year or even longer. After all, who is it that legislates in this country? Decrees of the Council of Ministers or of individual ministers, or the law decrees of the Presidential Council, regulate important matters that unquestionably demand statutory regulation. This is a classic example of how the executive branch usurps the functions of the legislative branch. And here I have not said anything as yet about the party's role, have I? I explained (and you must bear in mind that these are unfamiliar ideas in our country) that we must keep an eye on our statesmen and so-called experts, if for no other reason, simply because we recognize human fallibility; and the fact that institutional guaranties are necessary to ensure that the reform process, which was launched after a fashion but has since slowed down, will not be turned back. I mentioned how often unsupervised state geniuses have told us that there were mistakes, crimes, distortions and unlawful acts, which we had to applaud while they were being committed if we knew what was good for us! In other words, I presented all the customary arguments from the 17th and 18th centuries in favor of parliamentary government. The moment of being more modest in the 20th century than Montesquieu or Locke was not without its compensation, when I saw that the comrades were bursting with anger even from this much. This is where we stand, old man. For what I explicitly demanded was not even pluralism, merely tolerance, in a political sense the pre-1848 demands. But obviously even this was too much, just too much. Naturally, I brought up also the issue of the Hungarian minorities living beyond our borders. And I said that in Hungary, just as in modern societies in general, the most pressing problems arise concerning ethnic, racial, regional, generational, cultural minorities. Solution of these problems requires decentralization, self-government, goodwill, and tolerance.

Hírmondó: In your opinion, how has the Electoral Law scored on its test?

Gáspár Miklós Tamás: Look, I have the reputation of being a strict teacher at the university. But I do not think that I am exaggerating when I refuse to give the Electoral Law even a satisfactory grade.

First of all, everyone must accept the PPF's election mishmash. This in itself could pass, since even controlled and self-restrained democracy may have some merits. But the PPF's platform is too specific in terms of ideological commitment, and empty in terms of what has to be done politically. Moreover, it is not clear how much freedom of interpretation and variety it allows. We know that certain realities, and not like these, bind the hands of state leaders. However, everyone else, even people less opposed to some aspects of the system than you or I, must sign a virtual blank check for those whom they supposedly will have to oversee once they have been elected. Therefore I swallowed painfully when at last, after repeated questions, I brought myself to say that, Yes, indeed, why not, I accepted the PPF's election platform. Had I been elected, of course, I would have kept my promise. As it is, my life is that much simpler. I feel that I as a private citizen have regained my suspended freedom of action and thought.

Second, the institution of nominating meetings clearly favors organized groups. They are able to attract or sever their supporters and subordinates. Not to mention the fact that the chair did not prove unbiased, to put it mildly. Our opponents sat on the podium, at a table covered with red cloth, whereas we, i.e. Péter Balázs, the district party and PPF organs' "local candidate," and my humble self, sat below.

Third, the Electoral Law risks little. The National Election Presidium has to ratify the nominations, without appeal. The law does not even contain specific provisions as to who has to be notified, and in what manner, that ratification has been refused and on what grounds. Thus if László Rajk, for example, had won nomination, and if he would have been on the ballot had there been no cheating, as I have heard there was, the National Election Presidium could still have sent him packing.

Fourth, the law does not permit the candidate or candidates to campaign in advance. (Incidentally, this is something that Csaba Gombár objected to, on the above-mentioned radio program.) Then how the hell are the voters supposed to know who they are dealing with? Obviously, some interested voters will not attend, because they have no way of knowing that certain candidates will support issues that they favor. The voters attending a nominating meeting, with the exception of the people planted there, are buying a pig in a poke.

Nothing interesting happened at the nominating meetings where there was no truly independent candidate. They were more ceremonial and more meaningless versions of the usual, boring meetings.

Fifth, it is obvious that the nominating meeting, not the balloting, is decisive politically. And nomination at the meetings is by open vote. My dear friend, let us not forget that people in this country have lived in fear continuously since 1948, although today they have less reason for this. But who the hell knows? I personally would not underestimate the political instincts of the people.

Sixth, the complete confusion about the purpose of the National Assembly is well founded. Until now a seat in the National Assembly has been honorary, a reward to supporters of the regime. And "parliament" itself has served to create a semblance of legality. Just think of all the things that these deputies passed unanimously! The uninitiated voters regarded all this as a kind of grievance day at the local council, about elevators that do not run, bus stops that have been relocated, or the Patyolat (Laundry) Enterprise. One of my esteemed opponents, Foreign Minister Várkonyi, told the voters that there would be no lobbying there, and so did one of my supporters. Neither one became more popular for having said so. People have become accustomed to their inability to influence important issues. None of them has ever heard, and neither have I, unless something has escaped my attention, of anything being decided at the National Assembly, anything different from what the MSZMP Politburo in its wisdom has decided in advance.

Hírmondó: What actually happened at your nominating meeting?

Gáspár Miklós Tamás: Unfortunately nothing more than what we expected. On both occasions, at the second nominating meeting perhaps more so than at the first, the hall was "padded," as they say in the theater when tickets to a play are not selling, and soldiers and high-school students are admitted free to fill the unsold seats. Since "the representatives of workers" at institutions in the election district may attend the nominating meetings, the entire Markó Street (the public prosecutor's office, the courts, and all the rest) and the bureaucrats of the Ministry of Foreign Trade came, and so did white-collar workers from HUNGAROTEX whose director general, Mrs. József Szabó, was the other official candidate. Never mind that HUNGAROTEX, strictly speaking, was outside the election district. Furthermore, the activists and veterans of the district's party locals and PPF committees were also out in force. And every time I looked around the room, I recognized faces familiar from past periods of my life . . . (allusion is to police who have interrogated or otherwise "handled" him).

The uproar began when my colleague, Zsolt Krokovay, took the liberty to propose me for nomination. Next came about a dozen speakers who slandered me. Prominent among them were Mrs. István Szűcs, a member of the MSZMP Central Committee and first secretary of the 5th District Party Committee. She read my misdeeds from a card that had been passed to her. Incidentally, all her accusations were false. Mr. István Kardos, the well-known staff member of Hungarian TV, began to pry into my personal affairs. Even Foreign Minister Várkonyi went so far as to call me a warmonger (!) because I considered it my duty to bring up the question of the Hungarian minorities beyond our borders. Mr. Várkonyi was horrified by the fact that the Western press was covering László Rajk's nomination and mine, and because a few leaflets had indeed been distributed in the streets, demanding that the names of all four candidates be placed on the ballot. He complained that he was not getting an equal chance to win nomination. I felt sorry for him.

At the first meeting, when I had to or could answer the mostly hostile "questions," shouting held me up for about five minutes. There were demands that I be denied the floor and be made to shut up. As I stood there are the microphones and looked at the perspiring, pale and snarling faces, I felt a certain revulsion and sincere pity. When the yelling stopped, I was allowed to speak for a few minutes in complete silence. But then the leaders again keyed up the tenor and soprano. You probably recall that one woman became hysterical. She shouted "I can't listen to this any longer," and ran out sobbing. I wonder whom she meant, me or her colleagues? Probably even she does not know.

There was no yelling to deny me the floor at the second meeting, but I did hear such nice taunts as "Swine," "Idiot," "Traitor," "Provocateur," and so on. I was sitting next to two elderly women, probably clerks from some ministry. When they realized who I was, one of them said to me: "You know, the trouble with you is that we do not know you." After a brief pause, she added: "But then do I know Várkonyi? Who the devil does?"

When one of my friends started to speak about environmental matters, he was drowned out by shouts and forced to relinquish the floor. Fist-waving men of an athletic build and military bearings surrounded him and shouted, "Get the hell out of here, you bastard." A girl I know loudly objected to such organized disruption, whereupon another commando type threatened to slap her. Well, of course. They had filled three-quarters of the hall two hours before the start of the meeting, and completely intimidated the impartial observes who may have been present. What could these observers have seen of the whole thing? That a few young men who looked like intellectuals spoke in a peculiar manner, and that "the comrades," for some reason were extremely angry at them. The impartial observers may have even resented that a few of my supporters and I had caused such a horrible scene. Another thing we must not forget is how many models there are for spontaneous authoritarian behavior. After all, this did not begin today but in 1920, under the "Christian regime" that replaced outdated liberalism with corporal punishment and delivered the country to terrorist paramilitary secret societies and their chief shamans. One could indeed sense spontaneous opposition when the issue of conscientious objectors came up, a subject about which Foreign Minister Várkonyi proved to be shockingly uninformed. A young man, who had supported my statements on the Hungarian minorities, drew a line on the conscientious objector issue, and in doing so he obviously felt very patriotic.

And then the misinformation. When I stepped off the rostrum, all order at the meeting dissolved. I was surrounded by a group of people who had not been aware that there was anything wrong with the Hungarian minorities in Romania and Czechoslovakia. One of them frankly admitted that he had been ignorant even of their existence. One would have thought that a Hungarian from Transylvania might have evoked some sympathy even among the "padding," but some of them simply called me a damned foreigner. Xenophobia directed against Hungarians! Well, this was not the first time I encountered it. And so much for the Hungarian educational system and the Hungarian mass media. Just like in György Sándor's joke: "Dear Mom and Dad. I am here at the Artek Pioneer Camp. I have just won a contest 'Who knows the most about the Soviet Union and the least about southern Transylvania.' "

Hírmondó: Could you tell us something about your other public roles? In what ways did they differ from your present one?

Gáspár Miklós Tamás: Well, I was shouted down in 1978, soon after my resettlement in Hungary, at a conference held to commemorate the NEKOSZ (National Association of People's Colleges). There I managed to lock horns, for example, with Academician Béla Köpeczi, the present minister of culture and education. My audience calmed down in the end, although I had told the vilified former students of people's colleges certain unpalatable yet, in my opinion, essential truths. Thereafter I was active in, or the target of "public life" within the Attila József Circle and the Hungarian Writers' Association, and of course at the famous conference on the MOZGÓ VILÁG issue, held at the Law Faculty (a tape of this exchange was smuggled to the West and broadcast to Hungary by *Radio Free Europe,* trans.). I regret that Dénes Csengey, onetime secretary of the Attila József Circle, was not at the nominating meeting. Even when shaken out of a deep sleep, he is able to repudiate the standard slanders and libels against me, which for the past few years have contained the same unimaginative lies. The Ministry of Culture and Education took offense because a self-professed dissident had been elected to the circle's management. But only the ministry's representatives lost their tempers there. Thank God, not one writer took a pot-shot at me. Politically the committee meetings of the Hungarian Writers' Association are certainly more meaningful than the National Assembly's session, but, unfortunately, they are not public. However, there are people there who value freedom of the press and freedoms in general, and who are concerned about minorities, even though they themselves are not professional politicians. I can say that Hungarian writers have not yet lost their spirit of solidarity. Of course, the Hungarian Writers' Association and the Attila József Circle do not have much influence, and many of their members have given up the seemingly hopeless struggle. But these are elite organizations. You cannot send a hundred volunteer policemen to vote against Sándor Csoóri. I see that recently the party has been advocating art for art's sake, because it does not like the direction in which the writers are headed politically. We still remember the time when the party was urging partisanship in art, and the depiction of what it regarded as "public life."

Hírmondó: What is your opinion of the prospects for a kind of "controlled" and self-restrained parliamentary government in East Europe? What is the sense of such "legalistic" candidacies?

Gáspár Miklós Tamás: I am unable to say anything new about this. I agree with the opinion of István Bibó, (prominent political essayist, member of Imre Nagy's 1956 government, imprisoned by Kádár Regime, died in 1979), or of KOR (Committee for the Defense of Workers) in Poland. In spite of the coup and military dictatorship, Poland's Sejm comes closest to a parliament. There were surprises even at the congress of the Polish Democratic Party, a fictitious, pseudopolitical pseudo-organization. There is debate, and there are votes cast against proposals. Solidarity deserves credit for this. Before the imposition of martial law, even the Polish United Workers Party, which is Poland's communist party, held a congress that resembled real deliberations.

The power of the people is itself the sole safeguard of democracy. When the people are strong and active, even inert forms can be galvanized into life. The government's main endeavor in our country is to harvest the possible benefits of the economic reform, but without relinquishing an iota of its power. The outlines of a somewhat corporate system are evident. The enterprise councils that replace supervision by a central agency are strengthening the power of the party locals, because the latter obviously will pack the enterprise councils with their own people, and the party is the only organized political force. This is a significant change, but the question is who will benefit from it. It is also conceivable that the apparatus of the trade unions may be assigned a more significant role in the bargaining to reconcile different interests. Already now the one-party state is no longer the only possible employer, and daily dependence of people on it is diminishing. It is difficult to identify the power elite groups whose importance will be enhanced by the combination of a planned market and a simulated "real" market, but a change will certainly do no harm. At the same time, however, we see that the apparatus is resisting (its most prominent representative at present is Károly Grósz) and is attempting to blame every difficulty on the castrated reform.

The new Electoral Law enacted in 1983 is, in my opinion, a relic left behind by a vanished reform period and does not fit well into the party's present policies. Liberalization, if there is any, will not proceed in this direction, and so-called big politics will be excluded from it. You don't really expect that I will be able to stand up in the National Assembly and say: "All right, let us sign the Warsaw Pact, but first could you please tell me how much it will cost?" Nor can we expect that I will be able to propose repealing the Law on Subversive Activity, amending the Law on Associations, reforming the Press Law, introducing unemployment benefits, holding a referendum on the Gabcikovo-Nagymaros dams. In some respects the system's authoritarian features have been strengthened. Consider the recent "Vagrancy" Law, for example. Is this not a Hungarian version of the unemployment benefit, served with stewed onions, tomatoes and peppers? This law actually makes it possible to intern, suspend the civil rights of, and inflict corporal punishment on, persons who did not get jobs they liked or were qualified for. They can go and work in a mine, as the promulgating instructions specifically order. By reclassifying some offenses as misdemeanors, the competence of the police courts has been broadened. Knowledgeable sociologists have assured me that the "Vagrancy" Law is directed mainly against Gypsies. And it is certainly directed against the poor forced to the fringes of society. One would expect this to evoke real public indignation. But authoritarianism, I suspect, is too strong for that to happen.

Thus we can hardly expect to receive as a gift "from above" parliamentary government that, no matter how limited, has many features which may be considered genuine. However, we must not cease to spread the idea and to cherish its memory. So long as elections provide an opportunity to voice independent political opinions, we naturally may use them for that purpose. I can very well imagine however that the Electoral Law will be amended a bit. For why should those who wield great power lower themselves to where they must debate poverty-stricken nobodies like me?

A "legalistic" candidacy is of course a burden. It binds outsiders but hardly affects the insiders entrenched in power. But our candidacies have not been purely "legalistic" actions, in that we have not merely demanded compliance with the statutory regulations and the provisions of constitutional law. In the final outcome, we have attempted to influence the legislative process, although our attempt has been primarily a demonstrative one. After all, we ran on various specific platform planks! "Respect for the Law" for the most part is purely negative, a calling to account. But we have presented also some of our positive ideas, the ones that we could present under the established rules of the game. "Respect for the Law" urges compliances with statutory regulations of the highest order, but as I hinted in one of my speeches, the Constitution can be amended, that is the purpose of the National Assembly. This has been a self-restrained, democratic, political venture, be it ever so modest, whereas "Respect for the law" is essentially political and defensive. (Here, of course, I have primarily the "Respect for the Law" of Charter '77 in mind. Which does not mean that Charter '77, in spite of its mainly defensive orientation, is not several times stronger than the dissident camp in Hungary.)

Hírmondó: And what are the lessons to be learned?

Gáspár Miklós Tamás: There are some. In contrast with the nastiness that those who wield power demonstrated here, we have every reason to maintain our sober self-esteem. We are simply nicer than they are, since the air of freedom is less harmful to one's complexion than inflamed authoritarianism. And when I say "we," I have not only the democratic dissident movement in mind. For I have had the opportunity to see how beneficial it is, in the most obvious psychological sense of the word, when the participants of independent initiatives do something that they like doing. By this I do not mean to say that everything people enthusiastically want is good. Far from it! Especially since thousands of toadstools are growing in this excessively censored ideological semidarkness. Still even that is preferable to uniformed nothingness. For all these reasons, I believe we ought to propagate our principles and ideals far more openly and forcefully. Their least common denominator, I think, is the whole range of liberal democratic ideas. Analysis and protest are not enough. We have to specify what we want. We have to make understandable sometimes for our own benefit as well, what freedom is and what goals it serves. The fact that I happened to mention such things not to your average voter, but mostly to angry public officials, has undeniably been bad luck. But it has not done any harm to them either. They too need freedom, and would feel better under it. And they would then remind us not of the generalities of social psychology, but merely of the fact that a few of us have gathered together, so let us exchange views!

Hírmondó: Have these frank candidacies damaged the position of the moderate reform intellectuals?

Gáspár Miklós Tamás: No. This livelier (but, obviously only briefly so) political atmosphere can do no harm to them either. And perhaps "the comrades" will forget for a moment that they are being attacked. For there are other targets to attack, are there not?

NEIGHBORS AND THE WORLD

MURDER OF FATHER POPIELUSZKO
HAS IMPLICATIONS FOR HUNGARY

Beszélő 1, 1984,
unnumbered supplement

Popieluszko's kidnapping and murder is presented by the Polish authorities as anti-government provocation. Was it? It is possible. Is it true, therefore, that the government is not responsible for what has happened? That is certainly not true. It was Jaruzelski and his gang who had the Seym declare a law giving the internal security forces unlimited power to carry citizens off to prison. It was they who with their hate propaganda encouraged the violence used against the members of the opposition movement. It was they who sheltered the perpetrators of the almost 50 political kidnappings and several dozens of political murders that have become known since December 1981. It was they who declared, even after Popieluszko's murder, that they would persecute the human-rights groups formed to observe the abuses of authority and to publicly check the activities of the police. In a country where the leaders of the state turn their heads away to let their policemen, organized into gangs, perform the dirty work which they themselves do not dare do openly, the police becomes a state within the state and may, on occasion, even have the impudence to organize anti-government provocations. But only in a country like that.

Considering how much calmer the political situation is in Hungary than it has been in Poland at any time since the mid-seventies, the power of the police has grown at an astonishing pace.

In 1976, a decree of the minister of the interior exacerbated the sanctions of the police authority enforcement measures, unlawful to begin with. In 1981, the law enacted about state administration proceedings excluded the possibility for citizens to seek the protection of a court of law against decisions made by the ministry of interior and its divisions. In 1983, a governmental decree placed punishment for the violation of the so-called rule for press surveillance under the authority of the police. In 1984, again a decree authorized policemen on patrol duty to search the personal belongings of citizens when making identity checks on the street without giving specific reasons for doing so. The people in power have remained ostentatiously idle even when the police have been dissatisfied with these obviously unconstitutional authorizations.

In 1982, the minister of the interior and the Chief Prosecutor instituted no proceedings against the officials who had for three-weeks brutally harassed five contributors to a samizdat journal *(Beszélő, 4).*

In 1983, the Chief Prosecutor presented his intention in writing that he was not willing to start an investigation against the two policemen who had beaten up Gábor Demszky with night sticks *(Külön-Beszélő, 1).* On the other hand, the victim who had sustained brain concussions was — on the pretext of violence against the authorities — given a suspended 6-month prison sentence by the court (ibid.). The Justice Commission of the National Assembly did not even deign to answer the petition in which the members of our editorial staff drew attention to the fact that the government decree enacted concerning violations of the regulation for press surveillance by the police would contribute to the loosening of law and order *(Beszélő 9).* Since then a series of punitive sanctions have been meeted out using this decree, and the authorities make a show of the unlawfulness of these proceedings *(Külön-Beszélő, 2).*

The tactics are the same as in Poland. Just let everybody bold enough use his human rights and initiate something as an independent citizen to find out that he is at the mercy of the police. Still, the whole matter remains an affair of the police. It is not conspicuous and the leadership of the state does not have to shoulder the responsibility.

But it must shoulder it. The handwriting is on the wall. After Popieluszko's martyrdom no one in this part of the world can claim ignorance about what happens when the police are given a free hand to mangle human rights.

CALL FOR STRONG WESTERN OPPOSITION AGAINST SANDINISTAS

Demokrata, 4, 1986

By Gergő Deák

In Nicaragua the government refers to itself as Sandinista rather than communist. The communist groups that came to power as a result of the victory of the broadly based national rebellion which had written the name of the early twentieth century national hero Sandino on its flag, soon forced their allies, without whom they could not have overcome the wicked dictatorship of Somoza, out of power. They then created an extremely militaristic, totalitarian system, in which their party and the "popular organizations" on its leash give the orders in all areas of life.

The Nicaraguan communists who expropriated Sandino, the way Hungarian communists did the poet, Sándor Petőfi, do not let themselves be troubled any more than their comrades in Budapest when in the name of these national heroes, they eliminate the very freedoms for which they fought.

True, within Nicaragua and outside its borders the hateful memory of Somoza's dictatorship is still alive, just as post-1945 Hungary remembered well the widespread squalor and aristocratic arrogance that prevailed during the rule of Miklós Horthy. It is also true that the Sandinista government has three Roman Catholic priests among its members, a fact that is reminiscent of the fellow travelers who contributed, after 1945 and 1956, to the establishment and then the restoration of communist dictatorship in Hungary.

But how can this alter the fact that communist dictatorships are much more effective and cruel than any previous dictatorships, with the possible exception of Hitler's Nazi Germany? This is one of the reasons why a communist system, which destroys not only the political structure of societies it subjugates but also enslaves them and makes their economies uniform and deprives their citizens of the potential for independent initiative, is more resistant to internal efforts to overthrow it than any other dictatorship.

This is what makes the first communist government on the Latin America mainland so dangerous for all of its freedom-loving neighbors, even more so, because communist Sandinista ideology requires the support of "liberation movements." Exporting communist ideas of revolution and dictatorship, an important tenet of the ideology of the prime communist power, the Soviet Union, is already being applied agressively throughout Central and South America.

The size of the Nicaraguan armed forces is greater than that of all the other Central American countries together. Trainers and experts from Cuba, East Germany and other communist countries are already present in the country, as are experienced terrorists from Libya and the PLO, but while the Eastern Bloc and its Arab friends do not have to pay any heed to public opinion concerning the money and weapons they have been pouring into Nicaragua, President Reagan is denied a free hand in providing support for the anti-Sandinista rebels.

The Soviet Union, which supports Cuba to the tune of four billion dollars annually and whose leaders were never compelled to ask for parliamentary authorization for this activity or for their military campaign in Afghanistan, now masquerades as the protector of "weak little Nicaragua," shedding crocodile tears about American "intervention" there.

When will Western, democratic opponents of Reagan's Central American policies realize that only strong measures, not nice words or persuasion, are able to stop the advance of communism?

WARNING AGAINST APPEASEMENT OF TOTALITARIAN REGIMES

Demokrata 5, 1986

Neville Chamberlain, the Prime Minister of Great Britain, immediately before the outbreak of the Second World War, was famous for two things: his ever-present umbrella, which made him the favorite of cartoonists, and his so-called policy of appeasement, aimed at calming Hitler who was "thirsty" for war. After a series of concessions, this "policy of appeasement" led to the regrettable Munich Agreement and subsequently to war. If it was not clear before, it certainly has become clear to everyone since that time that concessions are not effective in pacifying aggressors and tyrants.

Recently, many people have tried to disregard this lesson. Demonstrations organized in Western Europe, mainly in Holland, Denmark, but even in West Germany at the time of the introduction of American cruise missiles to the continent, showed that many people live in a dream world, ignoring the fact that the period of "relaxation," the 10-15 years when the West made concessions, merely made possible the political and military advance of communist and more or less like-minded totalitarian systems.

In the last six months there have been numerous signs in the West of an unjustified proclivity for making concessions. In France, President Mitterrand played host to Warsaw dictator, Jaruzelski, and earlier failed to react to Khadaffi's breach of promise and aggression in Chad. Recently, the West German public noted with disappointment economic minister Bangemann's statement that humanitarian considerations should be separated from economic ones, that is that further loans and credit concessions to the Polish government are justified, even though the human rights situation in Poland has not changed at all. As for England, one cannot ignore the opposition Labour Party's demagoguery (blindness? irresponsibility?), demonstrated earlier by their demands for unilateral disarmament.

In a similar vein, for years there has been a need for decisive and synchronized Western measures against terrorist groups whose activities partially augment the policies of tyrannical regimes and partially use them for their own purposes. America has unsuccessfully urged the taking of such measures. The French are especially culpable in this area, but the Italian and West German governments also share in the responsibility. Their permissiveness led to the situation in which the Libyan dictator, one of the primary sponsors of terrorism, could believe that there were no limits to his adventurism.

It is a sad fact that certain Western governments are now ready to concur with an earlier Reagan proposal to apply economic sanction against Libya. The rejection of that proposal by these governments made the bombing of Tripoli and Benghazi by the United States necessary. The American administration is justified in accusing its European allies of indecisiveness and lack of moral fortitude.

The editors of *Demokrata* feel that the retaliation against Khadaffi's military installations was well-deserved. Those in Italy or in the United States who demonstrated against American military bases abroad or the iron-handed measures of the Reagan administration are unwilling spokesmen for the failed policies of Chamberlain at Munich. Their fate should not be so cruel as to have to learn first-hand that in a given situation, tyrants and aggressors will not honor cowardice and will not spare their persons or their countries, just because today they played into their hands.

In addition to cowardice and compromise another factor which plays a role in the condemnation of American actions must be mentioned. This is a masochistic, almost schizophrenic behavior.

What else could explain the action taken by the British union of journalists in sending a sympathy-telegram to Khadaffi? After all, did they send a similar telegram to the families of people who were killed, with Libyan assistance, on the TWA flight or at Rome airport? Psychologists may have an explanation for this kind of behavior, but under the circumstances it can only be characterized as disgraceful.

Not to blame the terrorists, not to condemn their instigators, but those who retaliated for these acts; to sympathize not with the victims, but with the murderers (after all, "they are human beings, too . . ."), what can one call such behavior?

The world witnessed similar phenomena a few years ago, when Israel entered Lebanon in order to retaliate for regular, destructive and murderous raids on its territory, and earlier, at the time of the 1973 Arab-Israel war. At those times, there were also many humanists, leftists and liberals alike, who chastised Israel, the original victim, for refusing to be a victim any longer. What they found especially objectionable was the fact that Israel backed up this refusal with a policy of iron-handed determination. If it were not for the fact that in 1973, and again in 1981, these outstanding humanists, along with the Western governments who were already then pursuing the policies of Munich, held Israel back, the Lebanon crisis would be over by now. Palestinian autonomy would have materialized (assuring, by the way, many more rights for the Palestinians than what the Hungarians of Transylvania dare dream of), and on top of everything else, the Syrian-Lebanese center of terrorism would have been eliminated.

In their masochistic self-hatred, the refined humanists of the West consider every problem of the Arab nations, Central America, Black Africa, indeed the entire Third World as attributable to the "crimes" of Europe and America and are ready to "do penance" for these "crimes" with extreme permissiveness, indeed self-sacrifice. At the same time, they ignore not only the fact that the overwhelming majority of problems in the developing world, especially in the Arab region, are in part the result of previous history, and in part created by local tyrants, but also that — as the potential or actual allies of the Kremlin — these tyrants can easily cause serious trouble for the West.

Well, if someone wants to destroy himself, let him, but no one has the right to endanger his country or indeed the entire democratic system of the West.

We, who have been placed at the mercy of a totalitarian system by the inevitability of history, need the Western democracies. Let Khadaffi's apologists, Reagan's critics, the "friends of peace" say what they wish, we here in Eastern Europe, in the shadow of the Gulag, having experienced the events of Budapest 1956, Prague 1968 and Warsaw 1981, know that the policy of Munich leads to slavery.

Freedom and peace don't need Chamberlain's umbrella but America's strength and Reagan's decisiveness.

SUPPRESSION OF DISSENT

KRASSÓ SUPPORTERS QUESTION
HUNGARIAN CIVIL RIGHTS RECORD

The following is an unpublished letter sent in English to the Helsinki Agreement Monitoring Committee. The original was circulated privately in Budapest.

The privilege of organizing the international Cultural Forum went to Hungary as a sign of recognition of its seemingly liberal policies, a respectable degree of tolerance, and a bearable amount of censorship, that is, of state interference in the exercise of spiritual faculties. This implicit praise of the Hungarian regime now turns out to be a trifle undeserved.

Mr. György Krassó, age 52, an economist, was recently — 22 November 1984 — put under police surveillance because of abuse of press regulations, i.e., for having written, edited and spread samizdat literature. Police surveillance in his case means having to meet on a weekly basis with officers and being forbidden to leave his flat between 8 p.m. and 6 a.m. to use his telephone, to attend public gatherings, and to visit public establishments such as cafes, sport stadiums, libraries or railroad stations. The violation of these requirements is punishable by a 10,000 forint fine or imprisonment for 1-60 days.

Mr. Krassó is an outstanding representative of the 1956 revolutionary generation. After the uprising, he spent 7 years in jail. In the subsequent years, he was harassed many times by the police for his outspoken ways and dissenting opinions and activities. He has edited and published important historical, political and literary works without asking for the censor's seal. He reported to the Helsinki Federation of Human Rights about the situation of these rights in Hungary. In doing this, he was only exercising the rights ensured in the third section of the Final Act of the Helsinki Conference, compliance with which you are appointed to monitor. Please consider this case before reaching any conclusion concerning the state of civil liberties in Hungary.

23 November 1984 Budapest, Hungary

G. M. Tamás, philosopher	András Nagy, sociologist
János Kis, philosopher	Ottillia Solt, sociologist
Miklós Haraszti, writer	Ágnes Hay, film director
László Rajk, architect	Sándor Szilágyi, literary critic
Gábor Demszky, sociologist	Ferenc Kőszeg, teacher
Konrád, writer	János Kenedi, author
G. M. Tamás	

Authorized copy

151

POLICE CURB UNDERGROUND
PUBLISHING ACTIVITIES

Beszélő 9, 1984

Respected readers and friends!

Szolnok Police Headquarters has fined Ferenc Kőszeg, an editor of the unofficial journal *Beszélő* 6,000 forints and graphic artist Tamás Molnár, a member of the Inconnu artists' group, 8,000 forints for violating the press laws. The decision was preceded by house searches and police interrogations. The police confiscated the duplicated cover of *Beszélő 8*, and its pictorial supplement showing Prime Minister Imre Nagy and his fellow martyrs. They also seized the Inconnu members' avant garde publications and political art work. The police action and the sentence, which also calls for destruction of the seized materials, is part of a series of measures taken against our "second public opinion."

Since the summer of 1982, the authorities have tried unsuccessfully to prevent the appearance of uncensored publications. They have resorted to harassment, searches, the confiscation of copying machines, typewriters, and manuscripts, and the levying of larger and larger fines. Even though they do not hesitate to use violence in public, they want to avoid a trial for violations of the press law and for political activities at all cost. They want to take care of those punishments, within the framework of violations of the rules which can be handled without a trial. Even though they say in writing that the illegal publications "exist only in small numbers," they seized 1,400 copies of *Beszélő*'s cover, and 2,000 copies of the pictorial supplement.

A trial would show the entire world what we already know here: the press law, as it exists in practice, is based on outdated regulations and contradicts both the Constitution and its Agreement on Civil and Political Rights, which is a part of Hungarian law, and the Helsinki Accords. This contradiction was previously brought to the attention of the public and the lawmakers in the seventh issue of *Beszélő*, when the editors applied for official permission to publish. Since then, the request has been rejected without justification. At that time, the editors also sent a citizens' proposal, attached to this letter, to the National Assembly's Legal, Administrative and Judicial Committee.

We ask our readers, each to the best of his ability, to declare that they do not agree with the punishment of our coworkers. We ask you to urge the thorough examination and democratic reform of the decrees which apply to civil rights.

Budapest, 1, May 1984

Respectfully,

Editors of *Beszélő*

POLICE AND COURTS WAGE ATTACK
ON INDEPENDENT PRESS

Beszélő Special Issue 2, 1984

Policemen from the District I station searched the apartment of Dr. György Krassó on 18 October 1984. The same day, they searched the car of a private businessman, L. S., in Budapest. On 19 October, they searched Tibor Philipp's apartment, and on 1 November, the home and office of György Gadó. In each case the police came in response to a "citizen's complaint" and "inspected the premises" without the required warrant. The above named individuals were questioned along with the office manager, L. J., and the printers, K. H. and Gy. Sz., some of whom had been questioned before. They were all accused of collusion in copying and distributing "printed matter produced without a permit." Gadó was also charged with writing articles which appeared in *Hírmondó* under the name Győző Ravasz and with taking part in writing material for the independent peace group Salom. Gadó denied these charges.

The large amount of material confiscated during the searches included not only photocopied articles but also photographs, prints, manuscripts and personal notes.

On 26 October, L. J. was fined 7,000 forints and K. H. 5,000 forints. On 30 October, L. S. was fined 7,500 forints and Gy. Sz. 5,500 forints. On 1 November, Dr. György Krassó was fined 10,000 forints. These penalties were imposed by the District I, II and X police authorities' regulation enforcement divisions. We can add that a 9,000 forint fine was imposed on Gábor Bouquet on 12 October by the District II police for distributing *Beszélő* on a city street. In one month, penalties totalling 54,000 forints were levied on these publications, also known as the "second public opinion," penalties equivalent to the average monthly earnings of 10 Hungarians.

In each case, officials cited regulation No. 21/1982/VI.15/MT, which places "violation of press regulations" under police jurisdiction. As early as September 1983, our editors turned to the Parliamentary Committee on Justice and pointed out the unconstitutionality of this law (see *Beszélő*, 9). Our readers need hardly be surprised that the committee did not initiate steps to revoke this law and in fact did not take the trouble to justify its stance to those who turned to it for help. Since then a whole series of penalties similar to the present ones have been imposed on us.

The goal is clearly to destroy the independent press without political trials or public scandals. However, the arbitrary restriction of civil liberties is illegal even when it is carried out discretely and without bloodshed. If the authorities can create a law whenever their interests dictate it, and if they can violate even the laws they themselves have created, the result will be a disintegration of law and order. And, being Hungarians and Eastern Europeans, we do not have to guess what the consequences of such a disintegration will be.

Beszélő does not intend to tolerate passively this strangling of the second public opinion. We turn for material and moral support to everyone who values freedom of the press and the protection of the law, to Hungarians at home and abroad, to European democratic trade unions, and to writers' and journalists' associations.

DISTRIBUTOR OF SAMIZDAT JOURNAL BESZÉLŐ ARRESTED AND FINED

Beszélő 11, 1984

Around 11 o'clock in the morning of 30 September, Gábor Bouquet was selling copies of *Beszélő* on Batthyány Square. A man who later turned out to be a member of the workers' militia summoned the police. When he returned with two uniformed policemen, Bouquet tried to disappear in the underpass, but when the police shouted "Grab him!" a passerby detained him. Bouquet was handcuffed, searched on the premises and, after the policemen confiscated the copies of *Beszélő* remaining in his possession, he was taken to the First District police headquarters. He was formally placed under arrest and for a while he was even locked up in a cell. He was questioned only hours later, when a plainclothes police officer showed up, introducing himself as "an expert on matters of this type." The apprehended distributor agreed to allow the police to go to his apartment without the procedure required for a formal search and agreed to the confiscation of the remaining copies to be found there. He was allowed to leave police headquarters around 5 p.m. His interrogation was formally recorded.

Two days later, on 2 October, Bouquet was summoned to the security room at his place of work. Two uniformed policemen were waiting for him there and ordered him to go with them immediately to the First District headquarters. Bouquet refused, saying that he was working and wearing his oil-stained work clothes. At this, the policemen handcuffed him. Before they departed with him, however, they made a telephone call, and afterwards they unexpectedly removed the handcuffs, instructing Bouquet to go to the headquarters after work. That evening the interrogation, not conducted by the expert who was present the previous Sunday, took a different turn. Bouquet was asked how one of the policemen who arrested him on Sunday got injured on the forehead. Bouquet stated that the policeman inflicted the injury upon himself when he hastily jerked out the handcuffs, and that the policeman himself acknowledged this at the time. "Why, does someone claim differently?" asked Bouquet. "That is none of your business!" the interrogator answered, and with this the questioning ended.

On the morning of 12 October Bouquet was again summoned — this time to the police headquarters of the Second District, where he resides. Here he was handed a decision by the Administrative Department of the Budapest Police Chief Authority penalizing him with a 9,000-forint fine or 30-day imprisonment for breaking the press laws.

Gábor Bouquet is a galvanizer at the Mechanical Measuring Instrument Factory. The amount of the fine is far more than his monthly salary. His address is 217 Vörös Hadsereg Street, Budapest H-1021.

POLITICAL AND EDITORIAL PROGRAMS

A MESSAGE FOR MARCH

Demokrata, Special Issue for 15 Mar. 86

O March, month of Hungarian renewal, season for national rejuvenation, when will you find Hungarians once again ready for action and filled with youthful ardor? Our problems are increasing, our troubles are multiplying: it is time for renewal. Who are the ones working for such renewal? Storm-clouds are gathering in the skies over Eastern Europe, and there is a foreboding sense of gloomy days in the unknown future. Are we prepared for them? Hungarian society is breathing the polluted air of false cliches and half-truths, while suffering from the cynical machinations of authorities who doubt the correctness of their own ways. The call of this society is like a cry in the wilderness, its bitterness is the subject of ridicule, and even its celebrations are forced and bitter. Our independence is a mirage. We are deprived of our past, robbed of our present, and our future is placed at the mercy of foreign powers. Was there ever an age when lies were more evident? Was there ever a time when corruption, deceit, and stealing became such an integral part of our national economy as today? Day by day, the quality of life is declining. Our waters are getting murkier, our croplands are being poisoned, the air is becoming increasingly polluted, and our perspectives are shrinking. Has Hungarian society of any other era ever experienced a general degeneration of life such as this? Have Hungarians ever submitted themselves to violent authority with such deep resignation and such helpless indifference as today?

But, after all, there is plenty to eat! (For the moment, anyway.) There are opportunities to become rich! (You and you, are you all becoming rich?) Never before have there been as many millionaires strutting (or lurking) among us as today! Go ahead, gorge yourselves, and forget your forefathers! Go ahead, flaunt your splendid new homes, and do not trouble yourselves about how you acquired them. Go ahead, believe that things are going well here for everyone who obeys the Party line and is not afraid of work. Do not look to the side where hundreds of thousands stand ignored. Do not look too far ahead either. Just keep driving yourselves and worry only about today.

Ah, we can rejoice! Today you are allowed to be uncommited. What an achievement. You no longer have to jump to your feet and clap in unison! Some might say that such neutrality is in fact obligatory when it comes to national integrity and the honor of society? This is the much-touted "public consensus" achieved between the authorities and society. The citizen is no longer compelled to be politically active. Those in power relieved him of this burden. For that matter, even work is not something everyone must do. If you are smart enough, there will always be someone ready to work in your place. . . .

But isn't there something missing? Is this a promising state of affairs?

Should individual and social conscience not be asked to finally speak out? Should the dismantled and ridiculed ideals not be finally reestablished? Should we not dare finally to confront all of the "realities" forced upon us?

Does "reality" encompass only the authority which opposes us, which is above us, or which is beyond our borders? Are we ourselves not part of reality? Are we prevented from seeking alternatives and taking advantage of new possibilities?

We must formulate the ideals and demands of these possibilities, outline their general contours, and point out the paths to their realization.

Storm-clouds are gathering in the skies over Eastern Europe, and above our heads, too. The embers of Poland are silently glowing, the residents of Prague are somberly listening. East Berlin must be surrounded by a wall so as not to become deserted by its inhabitants. Beyond the Királyhágó Pass (in Romania) a tyranny rages, and who knows when History will say, enough!

What will happen when the earth begins to move? Must the tragedy of 1848 be repeated, when Hungarians stood alone, deserted? Must the tragedy of 1956 be repeated, when the historical moment again found us unprepared and without allies?

We do not want a revolution. Such things always exact a heavy price. But we do want a peaceful renewal and a thorough cleansing. We want an open, truly democratic society in which we do not have to worship anyone as the eternal source of Truth and in which we all, people with varying points of view, beliefs and party affiliations, will be "the creators of a common good."

We want our nation to be itself and to be able to face its past and its present. As for the body of the nation, it should not be truncated, and the parts already detached by established boundaries should not be exposed to destruction. Inasmuch as we wish to dispute with anyone, we do not wish to do so for borders or territory, and not over events that occurred during the previous thousand years, but only for the living. Even for them, we would prefer not to dispute, but rather, if possible, to come to an understanding with those who have authority over them.

Our internationalism derives from the lessons of the historical events of March. This is not identical with the internationalism of our tyrants who are united in the service of a common master. We do not want to shake hands with the satraps in Prague, Bratislava, Warsaw and Bucharest, but with Czechs, Slovaks, Romanians (yes, Romanians!), Poles and the other peoples of East Central Europe. We extend our hands to them, even though we know that our handshake may only reach them through Munich, Paris or New York.

A new March Front is needed to establish the solidarity of all patriotic and democratic forces, but not under the dictates of a Communist party, not on the leash of the Kremlin. We need to consolidate even if it is without an organizational structure and lacking the forms of a party institution. We must attract democrats of the neighboring countries, who long for renewal the way we do. We need an alliance based on ideals which liberals and left-wing socialists, Catholics and anarchists could jointly espouse, and which are based on demands aimed at the totalitarian system that would make pluralism and democracy the starting point for all further change.

We urge, and in the following we provide proposals for, the drawing up of such a program. This humble draft will develop into a program only if democrats of varying convictions and interests pay attention to it by expressing their objections and suggestions.

May God grant that the 1987 Message for March be successful in its introduction of such a program.

15 March 1986

THE DEMOCRAT

Program For a Hungarian Democratic Renewal (a draft proposal)

A. CIVIL RIGHTS

1. We demand freedom of the press and of all means of mass communication and the termination of all forms of censorship, whether open, covert, or secret.

Police regulations restricting publication of press products must be abolished.

Restrictions on any kind of radio and television broadcasts in the country must be abolished and proscribed. A new press law must be created.

2. Those provisions of the law which restrict or make the exercise of freedom of speech, freedom to express one's opinion, and freedom of assembly and association a crime must be repealed. No one should be punished because he expresses his political views, so long as in doing so he does not call for violence, racial discrimination, annihilation, or for the commission of criminal acts.

3. We must reduce to a minimum those areas of authority exercised by police and administrative organs, wherein said organs are able to limit the rights of citizens by preventing appeal to the courts.

4. The right to work must be supported by the legislative recognition of the right to strike. General compulsory employment must be eliminated, as it infringes upon the freedom of citizens.

5. In defense of the individual and privacy, laws must be enacted to protect citizens against any dangers derived from the practice of electronic data registration. Laws controlling the census must be revised in accordance with the above.

6. The secrecy of private correspondence and telephone communication must be guaranteed. The authorities should be able to check private letters and wiretap telephone conversations only in cases of well-founded suspicion of violation of the law, and then only with an order from the court or from the prosecutor.

7. In accordance with the complete recognition of the freedom of movement, new passport laws must be enacted. Emigration must not be prevented by administrative methods. The term "illegally staying abroad" must be struck from the penal code.

8. Full freedom of religion must be guaranteed on the basis of equal rights for all denominations. The official obstacles facing the propagation of faith and religious instruction should be removed, and

the monopolistic situation of atheistic propaganda must be eliminated. The pressure and detrimental discrimination applied against religious teachers must be discontinued. The founding of religious schools on the elementary and secondary level must be made possible. State control over the life of denominations and state intervention into religious affairs must be ended. The legal status and the role of the National Office On Ecclesiastic Affairs must be re-examined. The denominations should be given the right to pursue profitable economic enterprises, and their state subsidies should be gradually removed.

9. The collective rights of nationality groups and ethnic minorities, including Gypsies, must be guaranteed by law. Voluntary efforts to preserve their traditions and linguistic cultures must be assisted.

B. PUBLIC LIFE

1. The leading role of the communist party cannot be a dogma for the entire society, nor a constitutionally declared basic principle, rather at most a result achieved daily in the practice of democracy. Even in this case, however, it cannot serve as the principle or legal basis for destroying other political trends or organizations, or for the denial of their independence.

2. Opportunity must be provided for the organized manifestation of every democratic political trend. Permission to operate must be given to all political, social, representational and professional bodies, organizations and movements (including associations which are like parties as well), as long as they do not advocate, or use, violence in achieving their aims, and they are not based on racist or Fascist principles.

3. The Patriotic People's Front cannot be the compulsory summit of social organizations, nor the compulsory framework for their operation.

4. Every citizen and organization has the lawful right to criticize the existing social and administrative order and to voice demands for its change. Legislation must be passed recognizing the right of the opposition to exist and regulating the methods of its participation in the work of parliament and that of local autonomous governing bodies.

5. The electoral laws must be changed in keeping with the above.

6. The work of the National Assembly must be reorganized. There is a need for more extensive and more frequent sessions, conducted under the effective control of the public. The principle according to which the government and individual authorities, their leaders and the cabinet ministers, are responsible for the areas entrusted to them,

must be enforced in practice. Governing by decrees must be reduced to a volume much smaller than is practiced today.

7. The independence, as well as the political and material responsibility of autonomous governing organs must be increased, both at the community and the county level. In personal matters, the right of intervention by central state organs must be limited. In politics, opportunities must be guaranteed for the local governing organs to maintain horizontal contacts and to undertake joint endeavors.

8. Institutional guarantees must be provided for the protection of political minorities against the dictatorship of the majority.

9. On the most important issues, both at the national and the local level, constitutional plebiscites must be used.

10. Constitutional courts must be established, for the purpose of defending legality together with, or instead of, the office of the Chief Prosecutor. The feasibility of establishing the institution of Ombudsman, so successful in numerous Western countries, should be taken under examination and advisement.

11. The genuine independence and greater expertise of the courts must be promoted. The administrative limits placed on the activities of lawyers (compulsory membership in lawyers' cooperatives, the list of defenders who can be called upon in political or military cases, etc.) should be discontinued. Statistics on criminal activities and the prison population must be made public in their entirety.

12. Increases in sentences prescribed by the Penal Code must be made the exclusive responsibility of the National Assembly. The concealed increase in the severity of sentences (the call for so-called "severe confinement" by the judges) is not in accordance with good legal practice.

13. The authority of the government during extraordinary circumstances must be re-examined, and it must be assured that, even under those circumstances, civil rights and constitutional institutions suffer limitations only to the degree that is absolutely unavoidable.

14. In accordance with the above and subsequent proposals, a new Constitution must be created, and the Civil and Penal Codes, as well as the Labor Code, must be modified.

Because of space limitations, the following areas which were covered in this program could not be included:

C. FOREIGN POLICY, NATIONAL DEFENSE

D. ECONOMIC AND SOCIAL POLICIES

E. CULTURE, NATIONAL HERITAGE

NEW SAMIZDAT PERIODICAL
PRESENTS ITS PROGRAM

Demokrata 1-2, Feb. 1986

DEMOKRATA greets its Readers, in the hope that he is also a democrat. Just like that, without any qualifier. In other words, he could be a bourgeois democrat, a Christian democrat, a social democrat, or even an adherent of people's democracy, just as the adherents of all those tendencies and their ideals are welcome to contribute to our humble publication. We wish to represent and realize on these pages a democratic pluralism which we would like to see in political life and for which we are ready to work.

We can clarify the various meanings and interpretations of democracy in the course of theoretical debates, but the precondition for actually realizing any kind of genuine democracy is the implementation of civil rights. As long as these rights are limited in Hungary, and as long as there is only one party and within it a small group which possesses a monopoly over "what is right," we feel that the sharing of views by democrats who differ slightly is at least as important as theoretical debates.

For exactly this reason, *DEMOKRATA* wishes primarily to become the practical organ of expression in the struggle for democratic rights. In this respect it attempts to introduce something new to the samizdat press. In other words, it does not wish to compete with the already existing serial publications serving the "second public opinion" (*Beszélő, Hírmondó, Vakond, Égtájak Között, Máshonnan Beszélő*). Rather, it proposes to augment and express in more practical terms those views which the other publications have expounded in theoretical articles, essays, and studies.

Our periodical will endeavor to be fresh and lively. We hope to provide our Readers with a new issue every month. And we will strive to attract those interested readers who are not receiving the above-mentioned publications or who find their content too abstract.

The Reader can influence us by supplying us with manuscripts, and even more so by providing us news and information. He can get all of these to the editors through our distributors.

Writings may appear in our paper either signed, under a pseudonym, or anonymously. Articles that are signed or otherwise identified do not necessarily reflect the opinion of the editors. This holds true even if the editors do not actually indicate that their opinion is different. However, we do not provide space for writings which are fascist, racially prejudiced, and chauvinist, nor for those which approve of violence as a means for domestic political struggle or extol common criminal activities.